MW01598396

THE DADDY I WANTED

Tia Mellor

Contents

Leaving her abusive father's house

Anna was about to light up the cigarette she stole from her father, after accomplishing the heavy chores that her father demanded that she must perform every day unless he will beat and starve her as usual, when she heard her father's voice again, coming from the house.

"Anna! Anna! Where's that little bitch," Mr. Walton shouted as he started throwing things around? He was beyond angry, everything wasn't just going as he wanted.

Upon hearing the emergence and the angry voice of her father, Anna knew that this wouldn't be good. She quickly put her cigarette in its pack and quickly returned the pack to where her father always kept it before screaming her reply to her father. "Father, I'm here," Anna shouted twice, so her father wouldn't accuse her of ignoring him, which she knew he hated.

"I've been calling you since 10 minutes ago, and you are in this same house. Do I look like a joke to you?" Mr. Walton demanded as he pulled Anna's hair and landed a heavy slap on her face, which immediately made Anna flinch and fell down in pain.

"I said," Do I look like a joke to you? " Answer, you little bitch," Mr. Walton rained a few more heavy slaps on Anna's cheek and kicked her violently, but Anna just endured the abuse because if she opened her mouth, this wouldn't stop anytime soon.

After a few minutes of slaps and kicks, Mr. Walton finally calm down as he caught his breaths and kicked the chair wildly in frustration.

But Anna was still mute, with her red swollen cheeks in her hands as tears ran down her cheeks. She quickly sniffed and cleaned her face because she knew that's precisely what her father wanted, seeing her cry and weak. If he turned around and saw her crying, he will continue slapping and kicking her. Apart from alcohol and cigarettes, the other thing her father derived joy from is seeing her miserable.

"Where's Maria? Is she inside her room?" Mr. Walton asked Anna, after calming down.

"She.she's not back from school yet," Anna stuttered as she wasn't able to fully form a sentence because her cheek was burning from pain.

It wasn't always like this, in fact, the maltreatment and abuse just started two years ago when she was 16 and immediately after her mother's funeral. Her once loving and caring father turned into a bitter man and started maltreating her because he believed she was the cause of her mother's death which wasn't in any way her fault, but he wouldn't even see reasons. He just wanted to digress his pain and grief onto someone, and she was the only one available.

January 2017 (Two years prior)

"Mother, No!! Please don't die. Please!!" The shrieking voice of a teenager could be heard everywhere in the hospital. But only the patients closer to the room could hear how miserable and dismal the little girl was.

"Anna, call your father," the dying woman who was lying lifeless on the bed opened her eyes slowly and muttered in a low voice.

"Mother, I've called him on the doctor's phone. He's on his way," Anna replied, hurriedly, while holding her mother's hand,

"I don't blame you, Anna, I decided to come and save you. Don't blame yourself," The woman replied and slowly closed her eyes.

pim pin pim

It was the sound that brought Anna back to reality, and she started shivering all over. She just lost her mother.

"Annabella! Annabella!" A slightly older man suddenly shouted, as he looked into the dead eyes of his beloved.

She's dead, and it was that bitch fault.

"Why don't you call me earlier?! she came to save you from getting raped, but you couldn't do anything while she was been beaten till the point of death! Why the hell did you go out in the first place,!" Mr. Walson shouted at his eldest daughter while the younger daughter cried slowly in the hospital.

"Daddy," Anna whispered, looking at her father with tears in her eyes.

"Don't call me your father, you despicable little bitch," Mr. Walton shouted as he gave his eldest daughter a huge slap on her face.

She is the reason the love of his life is dead! And from today onward, he will make sure that she doesn't know peace. Mr. Walton swore while looking at the dead body of his wife.

Present-day (December 2019)

Since that day, her father had told her that there's nothing like education in her life anymore and her only use was to cook, wash and also clean the house like a typical housemaid in her own biological father's house. If it wasn't that people always said she was identical to her father, she would have thought that she was adopted by him.

"Since Maria is not around, you better listen well to me now and get the hell out of this house before she comes back. I owed someone a huge sum of the money, I might never be able to pay him back and he in return also needs a contract wife, who will obediently stay in his house when he leaves for business trips and have his kids. You are just an additional weight in my arm and also look at how big and nourished you've become, you are just eating all my food and my precious daughter is even slimmer in compare to you," Mr. Walton asserted, looking at Anna with disgust clearly noticeable on his wrinkled face.

Yeah, precious daughter. Maria is the precious daughter, while she was just an additional weight. Is that not applaudable? Anna mumbled as she scoffed slightly.

"The man will be here to pick you up in a few minutes because I've already dethroned you to him and signed the necessary papers.

So, you better do well and be a good wife to him because if you ever come back to this house, I can assure you that your face wouldn't be as smooth as it is now," Mr. Walton threatened as he sat down on the couch.

Because he hadn't asked her to stand up, and she dreaded receiving another slap and kicks from him, Anna sat down on the tiled floor with her head bend low as she listens to him.

"What are you still sitting and acting like a cripple for? Do you want your future husband to meet you here? Go inside and pack the little rubbish you have and make sure that you hid all those marks on your body. And you better not take anything that's not yours else if I find out, you know what I will do to you," Mr. Walton retorted angrily when he saw that Anna was still motionless on the floor.

Immediately after his remark, Anna quickly dragged herself to her room to pack her clothes as he had commanded.

The only thoughts in her heard was....

She's leaving, she's finally leaving this hell. She was finally leaving her childhood home, which had become a hell for her since two years ago.

She was finally going to have a break from her abusive father.

Even if she was going to be a maid to the man and not his wife, she will gladly leave.

She just wanted to escape, she just wanted to leave this goddamn hell and God had finally granted her wish even though it wasn't the way she wanted, but she would still gladly leave.

After packing, Anna quickly scribbled some words in a paper as a letter for her sister.

Dear Maria,

I've left to become the wife of the man I've never met or seen because that's our father's wish. He owed him a massive debt. Don't look for me or be sad for me. I'm glad to finally leave. See you.

Your Lovely sister,Anna.

After writing the letter, Anna quickly hide it under the candle lamp because she knew that if it were to land on her father's hands, she wouldn't even be safe in her so-called future husband's house.

Going through the content in the letter again in her head, Anna tried to verify that she hadn't exposed too much to her sister. Because, unlike her father, her sister care, and they love each other as siblings.

If she's going to miss anything or anyone in this house, it's definitely going to be her sweet curly headed younger sister, who looked so much like her mother. Anytime she looks at her younger sister, she always sees traces of her mother in her eyes. They looked so much alike maybe that was the reason she was pampered by their father while she was abused instead, but she couldn't bring herself to blame Maria.

She was innocent and sweet, she was unable to bring herself to dislike her because their father was a wimp and alcoholic who only abused his eldest daughter and fawn over the younger one because she looked just like his deceased wife.

"What are you doing up there, do I have to drag you out? Can't you hear the car honking!" Mr. Walton shouted at the top of his voice when he saw that the little bitch hasn't come down yet and the man he who he had already sold her to was in their driveway already.

Is she trying to act stubborn with him?

"Anna!" he shouted again, and Anna quickly recollected her thoughts and ran downstairs.

"Father, I'm here, " Anna quickly answered when she was in his presence.

Mr. Walton was as angry that he was about to slap her again when he remembered that the old hag was still waiting outside. He reluctantly held himself back and looked at her with disgust.

"He's already outside, just go and meet him. And remember what I told you, don't you ever do anything that will make him send you back into this house. Else...." He dragged out as he looked at her work, in his cold eyes.

"As if, I even want to come back to this shithole," Anna mumbled under her breath as she held her small pack him her hands.

She doesn't have many clothes, her father burnt all.

According to him, she was just a little that doesn't deserve a penny from him. So, he burnt all her clothes, and the ones in her hands right now are the ones that Maria managed to save from her father's hands.

"Hey, come back here," Mr. Walton suddenly shouted at Anna. "Are you convinced you didn't take anything that is not yours?" He asked as he pulled the little pack from Anna and dragged it open as he searched for anything that might be valuable.

After seeing that she didn't have anything valuable on her, Mr. Walton turned back and went back to the couch, while Anna quickly packed her belongings again.

The only valuable thing she had on her was her mother's engagement ring, which was given to her by her mother in the hospital before she left this world. But her father didn't know about it, and he had never asked about it.

Departing from her home, Anna took a long glance at it and heaved a long breath.

She's leaving...

piiimmmmm pimmmmm

Car honks immediately brought her out of her daydream and she quickly hurried to where she was hearing the honks from to meet her soon-to-be husband. Leaving her abusive father's house

The contract marriage

Immediately she got to the car, Anna received one of the biggest shocks of her life.

He is an old man!!

The man who she would be spending the rest of her life with and also carry his children as her father had ordered was an old man.

He looked so old that Anna was sure that he must be over 40.

Cruel, so cruel!

Her father was so cruel to her.

She should have known that her soon to be husband wouldn't have any good attributes because her father would never allow her to be happy or be with someone that can make her happy.

What was she expecting? A young rich and handsome man? Pfft..

She should consider herself lucky that her soon-to-be husband was just old and not cripple or downright ugly. Because looking at him now, she could still see traces of someone who had been handsome on his face.

"If you are done scrutinizing me, I'd suggest you enter the car because I don't have much time at hand. Today is the only day I have to go to the registrar." The old man countered when he saw that the young girl who shouldn't be more than 18/ 19 was still staring at him.

Her father had shown him a picture of her earlier, telling him that she was his daughter and she's ripe enough for him to marry, and in place of the debt, he owed he will give his daughter to him in marriage.

He wouldn't have accepted if not because he knew that he had to start making kids, for he was a divorceé and his ex-wife didn't give birth to any children before she divorced him.

Upon hearing the urgency in his voice, Anna quickly entered the opened passenger seat because she was scared of irritating her soon to be husband. If she can avoid physical pain from him, she would do that because she didn't want to be abused and maltreated by the man she would be spending the rest of her life with.

"Your name is Anna, right?" The man asked immediately Anna was firmly seated beside him as he drove off.

"Yes, my name is Anna, sir." Anna replied in a trembling voice as she held her pack in her shaky hands.

"Don't call me sir, Call me Peter. I'm Peter Danish, you will soon be Mrs. Danish so you should get used to the name, " Peter said gently as he saw that Anna was trembling and wasn't comfortable around him.

He doesn't care for any state of mind she might be, all he wants is an obedient girl that would voluntarily stay in his mansion and give birth to his kids while he went for his business trips to make money.

"Oh..Oh kay Peter.., ". Anna replied again still trembling, and shaky.

Even though she was receiving any manipulative aura from him, she was still scared of him.

He was someone that her abusive father knew and sold her to, he wouldn't be of a good character. She was definitely sure of that.

"We are going to the registrar now and I wouldn't want you looking scared and forced, so stop shaking and put the goddamn pack you are holding onto in the back seat, " Peter let out when he saw that his soon to be wife looked like a puppy who was whipped and knocked out.

Anna hurriedly fulfilled his command and reminded herself to stop shaking else the man, no Peter...might hit her as her father does.

"Put a smile on your face too, you look forced. Do you want me to send you back to your father?" Peter asked, he didn't want an unwilling wife. If she was forced into this, he would gladly take her back to her father and demand all the cents he owed him.

Immediately Anna heard that Peter said he would take her back to her father, she flinched and quickly forced a smile on her face as she remembered her father's last comment that she mustn't come back to the house.

She can't, she definitely cannot let him send her back to her father..

She must act willingly. In fact she's willing to be anything he wants, a maid, slave, property anything as long as she doesn't have to go back into the hellhole she jus crawled out from.

When Peter saw the tiny smile on Anna's face he nodded, "That's better, keep the smile on every time. You will be needing it when you get married to me, " Peter advised as he pulled into the court registry car pack and died down his engine.

Immediately Peter alighted the car, Anna quickly helped herself down covering the visible belt marks on her neck with the shawl that she remembered to bring with her.

Walking slowly behind her soon-to-be husband, Anna prepared herself for the life she didn't know how it would turn out.

It's better to prepare for the worst. She had to adapt to it no matter how hard or dangerous it was, she had to accept it as her fate.

"Do you Anna Walson, Take Peter Danish as your lawfully wedded husband, in health, wealth and still death do you apart?" The registrar asked after Peter submitted the papers signed by her father.

Slowly brought out of her daydreams, Anna whispered her agreement and instantly sealed her fate with a single word, "Yes, I do"

"Do you Peter Danish, Take Anna Walson as your lawfully wedded wife, in health, wealth and till death do you apart?" the registrar repeated the wedding vows again to Peter and he immediately replied, "Yes, I do"

After signing the necessary documents and exchanging rings, Anna left the court registry with her new husband to the new home she would be staying with him.

The initial smile she had forced herself to put on while they were in the court immediately left her face when she was alone in a big mansion with her new husband.

"Can you cook? If yes, make use of the kitchen, I'm hungry as fuck, " Peter mumbled, as he looked of the outer suit and unbuttoned his shirt.

"Yes, I can, " Anna muttered in a low voice.

Cooking? Is that it? If he would only demand her to cook for him. Then her life just got easier because she had learnt different types of cuisine when she was working as a housemaid in her fathers house.

Cooking is just a hobby she had grown into apart from painting.

Anna immediately located the kitchen, when she got there she saw that there wasn't even much to do with it. The cooking ingredients in the kitchen were just eggs, bread, vegetable oil, carbonated milk, coffee beans and so on...

Anna quickly got to work and made sandwiches and some tea for her husband because that was the fastest food she could make with what she had at hand.

Serving the food on the table in a corner, which she regarded as the dining room, Anna stood beside the food gently because her husband hadn't appeared yet and she didn't know the room he went into.

After a few minutes, Peter showed himself in the room, "Are you done cooking?" he called out,

"Yes, I'm done, " Anna replied back, quickly when her husband came into the sitting room.

When Peter got to the dining room and saw that Anna only prepared a plate of sandwich he frowned, "Why did you prepare only a plate? Are you not hungry?"

Anna, who was already used to eating alone in her room, suddenly trembled when she heard the annoyance in his voice.

"I-

"Go and prepare yours too, I hate eating alone, " Peter interrupted dismissively before Anna could finish her sentence.

Anna hurriedly left for the kitchen again and came out with another plate of sandwich for herself and sat slowly in the opposite chair in front of her new husband.

"Let's eat," Peter announced when he saw that his wife was not seated.

Anna quickly held her spoon and started eating after her husband's announcement.

He said he hates eating alone, she had to take note of that and never repeat the error she just made because she was scared of what he might do to her when he was angry.

Would he be like her father and hit and kick her?

Anna shuddered at the thought and Peter could see her visibly trembling..

Is he thinking about what he would be doing to her in their matrimony room?

Peter stared at Anna through the corners of his eyes and saw that she was still trembling.

Is she that scared of sex?

Well, no worries he wasn't in the mood for sex this night because he had to leave for a business trip tomorrow and he wanted to take off as soon as possible.

But that doesn't mean she won't satisfy him sexually. No matter how scared she was, she still had to open her gorgeous mouth and suck on his huge load with her sweet lips.

Peter couldn't help but groan when he remembered how sweet and soft her lips were from the quick kiss they shared at the court registry.

He can't wait to have that mouth wrapped around his dick and stroke him till he shoots his cum deep down her throats.

Peter cleared his throat quickly when he saw that he was already getting hard at the thought, "Are you a virgin or not?"

Are you a virgin?

Another blinked immediately after she heard her husband's voice.

Virgin?

Of course, she's still a virgin.

She's just an eighteen years old high school dropout, and she barely leaves the house.

So where did she want to see a man that would shove his d*ck down her vagina?

The only sexual experience she had was when she rubs herself inside her room and fantasies about the men she reads about in the books her sister always do the pleasure of helping her get from the bookstores with the pocket money given to her by their father.

Apart from that, she's as innocent as virgin Mary.

She haven't even kissed or touch again a man before until today at the court registry.

"Yes Peter, I'm a virgin, " Anna slowly answered, as she looked down at her food and eat the last bit of the sandwich.

Upon hearing her confirming that she was really a virgin, Peter felt an unexpected feeling of lust run down his hair down to his crotch, he couldn't stop himself from imagining touching and exploring his new innocent wife.

Even though he won't have his ways with her now, he's going to make sure that he knows what her p*ssy warmth feels like with his index and middle fingers.

"You know what happens every marriage night, right?" Peter asked his little wife gently draped a serviette gently on the corner of her mouth and slowly licked his lips.

That mouth..

Upon hearing her husband question, Anna instantly shivered, "Y e... Yes, " She managed to let out, when she realized what he meant.

They were going to have s@x.

Her virginity which she had promised herself to give to the man who will cherish and love her will be snatched by the man she was sold to by her father.

Anna felt her eyes prickled with tears, but she immediately sniffed it back and acted as if there was nothing wrong.

Well, it wasn't that she wasn't expecting this because if she said that she wasn't expecting to have sex with the old man, she will be lying to herself.

Since her father said, her only usefulness to Peter is to give him children as if she was just a breeding machine.

Since it's just s@x, she will do it.

"Well, if you are done eating, go upstairs and freshen up. The master's room is on the left. Just take your bath and wait for me on the bed, " Peter said as he indicated to the steps in front of them.

Anna instantly stood up and made her way upstairs .

It won't hurt, I only have to calm down. It's better than getting beaten and treated like a slave.

At Least now, she can eat and sleep anytime she wants.

And it wasn't as if the s@x was going to last all night. She will endure it. Anna reminded herself under the shower after entering the master room.

'She's finally going to have s@x' Anna thought. Even though it's not how she had wanted, she's finally going to experience sexual intercourse with another human.

Regardless of how old he was, Anna was still excited because he was her husband and she better start getting adapted to the sex else she might never have a good sexual experience all her life.

It was after a few minutes when Anna took her bath and lay gently on the bed after wearing the red nightgown she saw on the bed earlier when Peter entered the master room.

He raised his head to see Anna's womanly figure on the bed, waiting for him and he instantly got hard at the thought.

"Do you put on the nightgown, " Peter asked with a deep voice, filled with lust and expectation.

Seeing that her husband was finally inside, Anna quickly turned and sat on the bed. "Yes, I did, " she replied to her husband's question.

She had presumed the nightgown was for her because it was new and it was right on the bed, so she had worn it after she took her bath.

She quickly thanked her stars for following her instincts, because she didn't know if he would have gotten angry and beat her.

She doesn't want to be beaten again.

Peter was about to switch on the light to see her almost naked body because he knew what the nightgown is made of, it barely covers anything. Since she was wearing it, he knew that her breasts would almost be spilling out because the nightgown wasn't her right size for he could see that she had an enormous breast.

"No, please leave the light off, " Anna said slowly when she saw her husband's action.

No! The light mustn't be on!

If not he's going to see the scars in her body, and he might not find her attractive anymore.

What if he's going to send her back to her father!

She can't go back!

She definitely can't go back to that house.

Peter, who thought she was shy because she was still a virgin, decided to leave the light off and moved closer to her on the bed.

When Anna saw her husband approaching, her heart tightened and as if it was pulled by a string.

Would he be hard on her?

Anna thought as she trembled

Peter smiled gently as he slowly unfasten the button of red nightgown his little wife was putting and as he heard her breathed a sharp breath.

Seeing her nervous and trembling, Peter found out that it made him even more excited and harder. Gently raising his hands to scoop her enormous breast, Peter found out that they are as soft as they looked. He rubbed his thumb slowly over one of her nipples and took the other in his waiting mouth as Anna sharply took another hot breath.

"When I learned that you are a virgin, I almost couldn't resist taking you right there in the dining room. But because I was to know how you'd look in this nightgown I restrained myself and let you prepare yourself, tell me how are you feeling, " Peter asked, but Anna only frowned.

This wasn't what she had prepared herself for.

She had thought that even if she was attracted to the old man, she would at least enjoy the s@x but when he grabbed her breasts just now, she felt like a frog was crawling on her body.

She has never felt disgusted! She would rather pleasure herself all her life if this is what it will always feel like.

"I said how are you feeling? Why are you mute? Don't you like how I'm touching you?" Peter asked suddenly as he halted his actions, "do you feel disgusted because I'm not young? Do you want a young man instead? Talk!" Peter sneered, but Anna was too scared to utter a word as tears gathered in her eyes.

He's going to hit her!

Or worse he's going to send her back to her father! She had to cooperate, no matter what. She had to take it.

"I feel good, I feel good," Anna quickly lied as she held her disgust to herself while trembling visibly.

"Hphmn! There's no rush. You will always be here when I come back from my business trips. You will learn to have my old d*ck inside you whether you are accustomed to it or not." Peter declared, suddenly losing interest in touching her.

But he doesn't want to touch her, which doesn't mean that he wouldn't still shove his d*ck down her sweet mouth and have her wrap her warm mouth around him.

At that thought, Peter instantly discarded his shorts alongside his boxes, and Anna couldn't help but gasp at how big he was.

He should be roughly 6 inches, Anna thought as she accessed the dark frame of her new husband's member.

Guessed age doesn't reduce the size of manhood, because she was expecting him to be around 4 or 5 inches.

Is he going to have sex with her now? Anna's heart skipped at the thought of having someone she couldn't even withstand his touch to be inside her. But she was surprised when her husband grabbed her right hand and wrapped it around his manhood, "Stroke me, at least you can do that right?" Peter mumbled when he felt the softness of Anna's hand on his dick.

Fuck! He was instantly excited and hard.

Anna looked at him, innocently, "I...I don't know how," she whispered in a slow and trembling voice.

Shocked and amazed by her innocence, Peter groaned harshly in pleasure "you don't know how? You don't know how to give a hand-job?" Peter asked as he looked at his new wife in the dark and saw that she was shaking her head as she trembled slightly.

"Find, then use your mouth then, wrap your mouth on it as you held it in your hands and suck on it, " Peter commanded,

Anna breathed down and slowly got up on the bed and gently bent her head and did as her husband commanded. Peter groaned hard when he felt her lips make contact with his crotch, " suck it, quickly, " he demanded as he held her hair.

.....In the morning, when Anna woke up, she noticed that her new husband wasn't in the bed with her. She looked around the master room sluggish as she was so tired from making her husband ejaculate multiple times with her mouth. And he even demanded that she swallow it all but it was so bland that she almost vomited until she reminded herself not to offend him.

Anna saw a tiny piece of paper and a debit card on the table and quickly grabbed it to see what her husband wrote on it. She found out that it was his mobile number and he instructed her to use the debit card for anything she wants, also asked her to get a mobile phone and give him a call.

She was finally getting a mobile phone, the thought of it only made Anna so excited that she immediately went into the bathroom to take a shower.

After getting a mobile phone and calling her husband with her new line, Anna found out that her husband wouldn't be coming anytime soon because he was running a contract for some Golden Gate Building. Which she had overhead when she was on a call with him.

Anna didn't know if she should feel happy or sad that she had the whole mansion to herself.

After three weeks of staying alone in the house alone with no one to talk to, Anna slowly starts getting depressed, and depressed.

She would have loved to paint a little, Anna thought.

Oh!!! Did she remember to bring her drawing book?

Anna instantly jolted her brain to recollect if she had remembered to take her drawing book with her but she found out that she might not have brought it with her and she suddenly felt a sense of loss washed over her.

Her paintings are her companions, they are just like her babies.

She wished she had a mobile phone when she was leaving, at least she would be able to contact Maria and asked her to bring her drawing book for her.

Maybe she should get a canvas, there are so many rooms here. She can set one up as her studio. Anna thought again.

But no matter what, she can't paint every time. She had to find people to talk to. At the thought, Anna brought out her new iPhone and went straight to safari to search for the most popular online platform to connect with people.

Joining an online platform

After surfing the net for a while, Anna stumbled on an online platform called Tumblr, at least that's what she thought it was pronounced.

At first, Anna decided to join as a single person but quickly threw that idea out of the window.

What if her husband got to know about it? Wouldn't that spell trouble for her?

Slowly she thought herself into not joining as a single woman but as a married woman, she will just talk to people and no other things. It's not as if she would be cheating on her husband right?

After feeling the required stages of creating an account, Anna's Tumblr account was finally created and she could see and add up people. She felt so happy because it would be her first time joining an online platform, So she was so excited that she kept on adding and accepting friend requests simultaneously.

*hello beauty *

Anna received a text from someone, immediately after she accepted his request.

Clicking on the profile, she saw that the person was as old as her husband, and she instantly blocked him.

What the hell!

She didn't join an online platform to meet old geezers, she's already married to one and she didn't intend to ever have another as a friend.

Maybe, she should just go and get a canvas and some other painting materials first then she would come back to looking for friends.

Anna picked up the debit card her husband left for her and left the mansion in blue jeans, a tank top and also sunglasses that she recently got so weeks back when she went to get her phone.

When she got out and finally breathed in the air of London, she couldn't help but feel the gush of loneliness wash over her again.

It is really nice to be outside among people. Anna thought after breathing in a new fresh air.

Even though her husband left his car for her to take anywhere she wanted to go, Anna couldn't drive so she had to order a ride from an app called Uber. Which she also recently found out because she had trekked to the place she got her phone some weeks ago and it wouldn't have been like that if she had found out sooner.

After a few minutes, a Red Toyota car pulled up in front of their mansion and Anna went closer to it after checking the plate number as instructed by the app.

"Mr. Christ?" Anna asked the driver in a low, melodious voice.

"Yes ma'am, Rapheal Christ, " The driver confirmed the name written on the Uber app, and Anna reluctantly entered.

With the way she was acting all cautious and hesitant, even the driver could be able to confirm that this is the first that his beautiful rider would be experiencing their services, "First time?" Raphael asked, bringing up a conversation to ease the stuffed atmosphere after setting the Google map to the destination the rider submitted on Uber.

"Yeah, First time, " Anna replied awkwardly with a stiff smile because she was shy and she wasn't used to talking to people.

"You can feel relaxed, the system is better than before and you will be safe if you follow all the necessary safety cautions set up by our company. This includes not entering the car until you confirm that the name and the plate number of your driver tally with the one on your phone, " Raphael advised since she was a newbie, and it's very necessary to take precautions and not end up getting kidnapped or something like that.

"Thank you, " Anna replied after a while, she smiled gently at the driver in appreciation.

It's very rare to see someone that's after other people's interest in this age, so Anna was happy that she actually met a very generous driver on her first time booking a ride.

Maybe she would always book from Uber until she learns how to drive. Because she didn't think her husband would want her to spend money on transportation after he left his car for her as transportation.

"Are we there yet?" Anna asked when she noticed that the journey was longer than she expected.

"No ma'am, you are going to the Diva's painting shop, right? We will get there in a few minutes, " the driver replied after checking the map again.

Anna, who had no idea how far the painting shop she found online, instantly became bored and decided to check her Tumblr if she had received new friend requests.

Scrolling through the new friend requests she had just seen, Anna blocked some and accepted some because honestly most of them weren't even what she wanted.

In fact, she didn't know what she wanted.

In her mind, she had thought that she would meet the kind of men she always read about in the romantic books that Maria always got for her in the book store but she was very disappointed until she came across a profile.

Dark, 30, single, and ready to make friends. Don't add up if you are not naughty.

Because of the last write up and also because of the handsome display picture she saw on the man's profile, Anna decided to add up.

Naughty? Is she naughty? Anna thought as her cheeks instantly heats up, and she had to fan herself with her fingers in the Air-conditioned car.

"Are you feeling okay, Ma'am?" Raphael asked when he saw her action, he was genuinely concerned because he could see that her cheeks were getting red. "Are you comfortable?" he asked again.

"Yeah, I am. Thanks for your concern," Anna quickly mumbled when she saw that she was overreacting.

Okay fine, she's definitely not naughty but isn't it just an online chat?

She can be anything she wants since she wouldn't be seeing him. She thought but after sending a friend request, she saw that the man wasn't online and he couldn't accept the request at the moment.

When Anna looked up, they already got to the painting shop. So she quickly paid the driver and thanked him for his advice then went inside the shop.

When she got to the canvas section, she saw that there were different types of cotton and polyester canvas and she was suddenly confused about which one to buy and also the price range was also hefty.

After selecting one with a medium price, she moved to the brush sections to get painting brush, rollers, spray gun and so many others. When she was finally done shopping, she requested another ride as she pushed the cart to pay for her goods.

When Anna got back home, she set up her studio in a room that wasn't far from the master's room after so much consideration. Totally forgotten about her phone or the fact that she was expecting a particular man to accept her friend request, Anna delved into painting.

Immersed in creating the image in her mind, Anna didn't know when the time was fast spent and it was already the evening before she could finally drop her brush and look at what she created.

It was beautiful, Anna thought as she looked at her paint.

It was a picture of a young girl, with her body filled with scars as she was about to accept the outstretched hand of a man even though the man's hand was filled with thorns.

While she was admiring her work, Anna's stomach churned with hunger. That was when she recalled that she hadn't eaten since she left to get a new canvas, so she quickly went into the kitchen to prepare pasta for dinner.

It was when she was eating that she got a notification on her phone that says that her friend request had been accepted by the profile which says "Jackson Mikealson". and she also saw that she had a pending request from another Mikealson, named Jacob.

She instantly became baffled, is he the same person? Why did he open multiple accounts? Anna thought as she ignored the other friend request as the person on the display picture was still the same person until she received a message from her new friend "Jackson Michealson"

Jackson Mikealson: accept the other account pending request, so we can chat better.*

Is the other account private? Is that why he wanted her to accept? Anna thought strangely and reluctantly accepted the request and she finally returned his chat.

Anna Danish: Accepted. Hi?* Anna typed on her phone as she patiently waited for a reply while she dropped her dish in the kitchen and went to take a shower.

After bathing and cuddling under her bed with a huge duvet around her naked body, Anna decided to open her Tumblr again as she already saw that she had different messages from "Jacob" and also from "Jackson".

Why is he chatting with her on two different accounts?

Is that like a new social media thing? Anna thought strangely as she opened the messages.

They come in pair?

Anna first opened the message from Jackson because he was the first person she added by herself, and also because she thought that he was also the same person as Jacob.

Jackson: So Anna right, or is this like an online name?* that was the message she read when she opened the chat, she couldn't help but chuckle lightly to herself.

Anna: No it's not, that's my name. Is your own an online name?* she replied as she chatted back.

Jackson: Definitely not. So Anna, why aren't you replying to my brother's message? In case you don't know we came in pairs. If you don't want to chat with him, we will have to stop chatting too.*

Brother? Came in pairs? Wait! Are they twins?

OhmyGod!

Anna shivered slightly in excitement, she had always wanted to chat with twins, and talk to them at the same time. She quickly went to check Jacob's profile, and she found out that they were really twins, but apart from that, she wasn't able to find out much about them.

Anna: You guys are twins? I had no idea, I literally thought it was you chatting me up with another account. Yes, I'd love to know you guys, * Anna quickly replied to Jackson's chat as she went to open Jacob's message.

Jacob: Hello pretty lady, don't tell me you are already wooed by my brother.* that was the message Anna was when she opened Jacob's chat, and couldn't help laughing out loud.

Okay, so they are really twins and Jacob definitely got to be the playful one because he ended his chat with a smirk emoji. Chatting with them differently was so hard but because she needed the company, Anna put up with it until Jacob suggested a group chat between them.

Anna: Can I really chat with you guys here together?*Anna texted immediately she was added to the group chat.

She didn't know there was something like that, a group chat. Since the platform was the first online platform she ever joined.

(Found out that it was actually tasking to write in a way to show that they were typing, so I'm just gonna write it like a normal conversation. But please bear it in mind that they are chatting online and not in real life. If it's confusing, let me know in the comment section so I can change it because the trio will still chat online so many times in the book. Thank you.)

"Of course, you can chat with us here together, that's why I suggested that," Jacob typed immediately on his phone when he saw her strange question.

Is she new to Tumblr?

How did Jackson find a newbie?

"Are you sure she would be up for it, " Jacob quickly texted his brother privately.

"Well, I stated that I don't want a saint though. I checked her profile before accepting, she's 18 and she's married." Jackson replied to his twin brother's chat.

"18? And already married? Is that not like the high school age range?"

"Yeah, but she stated that she's married and not single." Jackson replied, "let's not keep her waiting, we should know if she's up for it or not."

"Sure," Jacob replied and called Anna on a video call suddenly to verify that it wasn't a catfish account because he had never met a married 18 years old girl before. Most 18 years old girls he knew are probably in high school about to write their college exams, or in the club shaking their asses off to make money.

When Anna saw the video call, she became skeptical.

Should she accept the video call or not?.

But later decided to accept the video call since she had to verify that they were real people too. Immediately she accepted, she was stunned to see two gorgeous identical dark-skinned guys on her phone screen.

She was so amazed that she didn't realize that they were also checking her out.

"She's breathtaking, " Jacob quickly chatted his brother up with a smirk emoji.

"I can see that, I also find her attractive, but let's not get our hopes up. What if she's not into that?" Jackson replied.

"Are you guys still here?" Anna asked, after looking at the twins to her satisfaction.

"Sure dear, we are still here. Nice hair and eyes you've got there. It's very beautiful, " Jacob commented while they were on a video call, and Anna couldn't help but smile.

"Look bro, she also has an enchanting smile, " Jacob announced as he was already attracted to the young girl his brother had found online.

He couldn't wait to pull her brown gorgeous curly hair and watch her stare at him with those soulful brown eyes.

"I can see that, "Jackson replied as he looked at the girl on his iPhone screen.

She was really beautiful.

"Are you really married, or is that like an online something, ?" Jackson asked cautiously, he had met so many females that love role-playing as a married woman because of the fantasy of infidelity.

But he never found it amusing a bit, it was even because of her marital status that he delayed accepting her request.

He wanted a single woman that would be ready to sign the contract after their former sex slave contract ended.

Yes, he and his brother are DOMs that keep a willing sex slave.

"Yes, I'm married," Anna replied after a few minutes, she was totally baffled.

Do people lie about that too?

She would never lie about her status though, she was married,but she was only looking for online friends maybe perhaps....not just friends but online sex partners that she can sexchat or phonesex with.

After a few weeks of getting to know the twins, Anna found out about their weird fetish of saying harsh words and commanding her to bend to their will. They even called themselves her masters and told her that she is their sex slave.

Anna couldn't help but get excited and horny anytime she remembered how they'd tell her to slap herself on video call and moan out their names like a sex slave.

At first, she didn't find it amusing because year's if maltreatment and abuse from her father had given her congenital insensitivity to pain and she couldn't feel any pain. But she later got used to slapping herself and spanking her own ass anytime they asked her to do it on video call.

They tried all different types of sessions online except the ones that can't be done online and the twins had repeatedly invited her over to their house but she kept on declining because she didn't want to be unfaithful to her husband.

Because if he finds out and sends her back home, her father will make sure that her life becomes a living hell!

"Are you still going to refuse our invitations? Don't you want our dicks to fill your holes as you've always imagined?" Jackson texted, he was now very comfortable chatting with Anna and he couldn't wait to have her looking at him as she wraps her mouth in his dick while his brother fucks her from behind.

"Come on, Anna. Didn't you say that your husband is away? We can send you back home before he arrives from whatever shithole he crawled into leaving a beautiful woman like you unattended to." Jacob flirted, adding to his brother's remark.

When they first met Anna online, he was away on a business trip to France while his brother was in London so he wasn't really hungry to see her. But now that they were both in London, they couldn't wait to possess her and made her accept that she likes me when they talk dirty to her.

"Fine, I will come around. But it's only for a day because my husband didn't say when he will be back and it can be anytime, " Anna finally agreed to see the twins.

It's just for a day. What could possibly happen?

She just had to come back home and act like she never met them.

"Don't worry, little girl. You are safe with daddies, " Jacob texted excitedly when he saw her confirmation text.

Finally, they would meet their little slave.

"Can you drive? If not, can you text your address so we can order someone to pick you up, " Jackson typed. He was always the calm and sane one out of the twins.

"No, I can't drive. But don't worry about picking me up. Just send your address and I will come, " Anna quickly replied.

"Okay, no problem, " Jackson texted their mansion address to Anna after she convinced them that she had really come and she wasn't leading them on.

....

When Anna woke up the next day, she decided to input the address on Google Maps to see how far it was from her residence. Anna had refused to allow the twins to pay for her ride because she didn't have a bank account, and the only card she was using belonged to her husband. She was scared too scared that he would be notified of every transaction.

What would he think when an unexpected sum of money entered his account? Wouldn't he be suspicious of her?

After she was done with the necessary things in the house, Anna booked a ride and input the address of her new masters, or daddies as they like to be called.

On getting to the address, she was escorted inside the enormous mansion which was thrice her husband's mansion by a man who introduces himself as the housekeeper but she couldn't remember his name.

The housekeeper said his master was already waiting for her and he directed her into the mansion.

Immediately they got into the mansion, the housekeeper left her on her own and gave her some directions to follow.

No matter how horny and excited she was about meeting her new-found masters, Anna was still a little scared because she has always been shy and an introvert.

I will just blame this on loneliness and depression. Anna said to herself as she opened the door to the room the housekeeper directed her into.

Immediately she opened the door, Anna's eyes widened in shock when she finally saw the twins.

Meeting her new daddies

"Oh, so this is our beautiful and shy little s*lex slave," Anna heard, who she believed should be Jacob because of the sexy remark, and how his eyes were twinkling.

"She's not our slave yet, "Jackson countered and cautiously threw a piece of the document on the table before Jacob got to Anna.

"But she's still our sex slave, aren't you, darling?" Jacob said, as he moved closer to Anna and gently whispered in her ears. He was loud enough for Jackson to hear and low enough to send shivers down Anna's spine.

"I...I am," Anna managed to breathe out, as she trembled slightly. This time not for fear that they were going to hurt her, but for excitement and desire.

"See, she already said she is, "Jacob countered as he slipped his hand around Anna's waist, and led her to one of the chairs in the sitting room.

Immediately Anna sat down, Jackson allow his eyes to freely roam around the body of the woman they had been having phone sex, and BDSM sessions with, and he couldn't help, but suddenly feel excited.

"Are you really 18?" Jackson asked as his eyes settled on her breasts. He couldn't stop his eyes from staring more at the beautiful folds that were secretly hidden behind her blouse.

"Yeah, I'm eighteen. March 20," Anna answered defensively.

"Well, then. I'd like you to go through the form and sign if you are in," Jackson said to Anna and pushed the papers in front of her.

Consensual form was written boldly on the document when Anna picked up the papers.

Did they want to sign that she agreed? Is that what the papers are for?

Anna thought as she read the pages of the form, slowing and agreeing in her mind until she reached a part where it said she would only belong to them.

She was married, why would she belong to another man?

She would just ignore that, she definitely couldn't refuse to sign the form because she was married.

Wouldn't she be gone by tomorrow? She would just forget about them. Anna told herself as she gently put down her signature on the piece of paper.

"Well, looks like you really want to be treated like an s@x object, don't you?" Jackson asked as he moved closer to the seat Anna was sitting on, and gently rubbed her thighs.

With the contact of his firm hand on her thighs, Anna almost groaned out loud in pleasure.

Why was she so attracted to these brothers?

"When he asks you a question, you should try to answer immediately because if he gets angry he might punish you," Jacob whispered into Anna's ears as he used his tongue to slowly trace her earlobe.

Anna choked out the moan in her throat as quickly answered, "Yes, I want to be treated like a sex object,"

Moving his hand gently slowly from her thighs down to the V of her leg, Jackson flashed a half-smirk at Anna, "You are so slutty, how many months have you been married to your husband? How many times have he touched you?" Jackson asked in a cold and dangerous voice, but Anna found it so sexy she couldn't help, but tremble again.

Will they continue if she told them that she's a virgin?

And the only sexual experience she had ever had was when her husband made her put her head around his dick and make her suck it?

"He. He hasn't touched me before?" Anna said slowly when Jackson's hand suddenly brushed her panties.

"Oh, really? Then who has?"

"No. No one has, except me." Anna answered innocently.

She's a virgin.

"Jackson, I told you she's still a virgin," Jacob said excitedly to his brother.

"Are you a virgin? Considering how slutty you were on the phone, I didn't believe him," Jackson asked, rubbing her clit through her panties. Her brown eyes turned deep brown from pleasure.

Yes, she wanted this.

She really wants to be trapped between them and let them take her innocence away. Until she suddenly remembered that her husband knew that she was a virgin, and that was also why he hadn't touched her that night. Saying that they had all their lifetimes, and he will wait until she's willing.

No, she can't allow them to fuck her pussy. Her husband would know about her infidelity and send her back to her father. She asked her head violently at the thought that Jackson almost thought she was denying been a virgin until she spoke, "Yes I am a virgin,"

"You see, tell you." Jacob said again. But by this time, Jackson had already slipped a finger inside Anna's dripping core. It was Anna's groans and sexual moans that made Jacob realize that his brother was already halfway inside their little slave's pussy.

Impatient now, aren't we?

Immediately Jackson put his middle finger inside Anna's core and found how tight and wet she was, he felt his member tighten in aspiration.

She really was a virgin.

This was the first time they would be having sex with a virgin. Most of the time, it's usually girls that love sex and wants to be used like a slut that they continually search for.

But Anna was even more slutty than those girls, she always does everything they asked her to do on the phone. He could remember when they had asked her to blindfold herself and spank herself while she muttered their name. She had done it so well that they both couldn't help but wank on her slutty actions.

"Then, how come you are so slutty," Jackson asked as he removed his middle finger from her wet pussy, and gently pinch her clit while Anna moaned out slowly from pleasure.

Jacob was smirking at Anna's back, he was looking at how gorgeous and sexy she was as she moaned out loud.

He could feel his dick tighten in excitement and expectation.

"You can't wait to have us inside you, right?" Jacob whispered again in Anna's ear and made her shiver at his deep baritone voice. She looked at him and gently begged him with her eyes.

She really couldn't wait, she couldn't wait for them to fill her holes. She just wanted to feel like a sex slave and nothing more.

Looking at her breathtaking eyes, and how they were staring at him, Jacob was so hard that he couldn't help but slap her cheeks gently.

Instantly her pale white cheek reddened, Anna who was expecting to feel fear because of how scared she was always when someone raised their hand to strike, or when they yelled at her was suddenly confused.

Why did she find this painful and pleasurable at the same time? She thought she was already immune to slaps, and she doesn't feel pain anymore.

But when her cheeks were slapped by Jacob, she could feel her cheek tinge in pain, and then it slowly turns to pleasure.

Suddenly, she wanted to be slapped more by him.

No, she couldn't wait to be slapped more by him.

What is this? Why is she feeling like this??

This is not her!!

"Why did you accept our invite? Tell us again," Jacob asked Anna, as he slapped her already swollen and red cheeks.

"Because I want you guys to treat me like a sex slave," Anna gulped and said the first thing that was on her mind.

They were turning her on so much. She didn't expect that she would have been so wet and horny immediately when she got here.

"I know you are definitely expecting this, that was why you came, right? To be used and treated like a dirty whore, right?" Jacob asked and slapped her cheeks again.

Yes, that was why she came but... this was more than she expected..... because they were so explicit with her and she was loving every bit of it.

Shall *we* play a naughty game?

"Talk," Jacob's voice became authoritative and cold. "If you don't answer my questions immediately, I will also punish you. Jackson is not the only one that gets angry when his questions get delayed," he added, grabbing Anna's cheek as he forced her to look into his eyes.

"Yes, I was.... expecting this," Anna choked out when she wasn't able to ignore the effects they were having on her.

"Tell us, what else were you expecting?" Jackson asked in his sexy voice as he inserted his hand inside Anna's skirts again.

This time, he didn't insert his fingers inside her pussy, instead he gently dragged her panties down her legs.

"Hmm, pink. Typical teen. Aren't you?" Jacob mumbled when he saw Anna's panties.

"Yes," Anna gasped at the male species in front of her, who looked very identical with their broad shoulders, and how firmly the t-shirt on them was hugging their skins. She moved her eyes to slowly appreciate their tanned skins, firm lips, and soulful blue eyes which were slowly dragging her into the thorns of Infidelity.

Presently, she wasn't able to bring herself to think about the fact that she was a married woman or the fact that she was a virgin.

She honestly wants to be fucked and slutted out by them.

"What else is also pink? Your pussy?" Jackson asked before he slid his hand between her legs to spread them apart so that her vagina could be seen by him and his brother. The action made Anna feel like a slut, a client was checking out. The thought made her pussy tremble in excitement, and she almost moaned out again.

Stroking his finger gently against her folds, Jackson let out a satisfied groan when he saw how wet she was.

"You are so ready, aren't you?" He muttered as he brought out his fingers and plunged them inside Anna's mouth. Anna almost choked at the sudden invasion until she tasted her juice, and gave out a low moan of pleasure.

"Shall we play a naughty game?" Jacob asked, his voice filled with naughty intentions as he stood up, and moved toward the drawer in the room. With a smirk on his face, he brought out a blindfold and cuffs.

Immediately Anna saw the blindfold and cuffs, she instantly recalled how much she pleasured herself that day they asked her to blindfold and spank herself on a video call.

Is that what they want to do to her now?

"Do you remember when we asked you to blindfold yourself and spank your slutty little ass?" Jacob asked as his eyes ogled Anna's exposed pussy, which was dripping with moisture from her juicy vagina. "How about you close her legs first, Jackson? I can't think when I look at that pink and dripping pussy" Jacob groaned out in a deep sexy voice.

"You are the one who wants to play a game," His brother shrugged off and chuckled slightly.

"Anna, don't you always want to play a naughty game with daddy?" Jacob mumbled slightly as he walked closer to Anna, with the blindfold and cuffs in his hand.

Excited by the feeling of pleasure to come, Anna innocently replied in a low voice, "Yes, I want to play with daddy,"

Smirking with his eyes full of mischief, Jacob gently brought Anna's hands together and cuffed it with the cuffs. The passion ignited inside Anna's core, immediately she realized she was completely under their mercy.

"Now, I'm going to cover your eyes with this blindfold," Jacob asserted, after cuffing Anna's hands. When they successfully blindfolded her, the two brothers moved closer to Anna and started touching her body simultaneously.

She couldn't see, she could only feel. She could feel their hands on her waist, neck, clit, and breasts. It was all so overwhelming, she didn't know when she started moaning loud and telling them that she couldn't wait to have them inside her.

"Say that again," Jackson muttered in a deep sexy voice as he gently used the finger that was inside Anna's vagina earlier to stroke her bottom lip, feeling her soft lip while Jacob folded her breasts and kissed her neck.

"I...can't..."

Anna couldn't finish her words when she suddenly felt her left nipple being pinched roughly, the burning sensation in her disappears as another takes its place in her lower regions.

This is absurd! This was the first time she would be meeting these brothers, and her body wasn't even hers to control anymore.

"You can't do what? Tell your daddies what you want, " Jacob mumbled in a sexy hoarse voice as his lips slowly traced Anna's earlobe, and his hands gently folded her breast while he pinched her nipples again roughly, making her moan out again in pleasure.

"I can't wait.... to have you guys deep inside me," Anna finally admitted to her naughty desires when she saw that she couldn't resist the pleasure anymore.

Jackson smirked slightly, "Don't worry, little slut, you will get you more than you desire." The brothers shared a look and Anna suddenly felt her vagina release another moisture of juice as her body tingled due to the sexual tension building in her body.

"Damn, your breasts are so soft, turn around, let me have a taste of them," Jacob ordered, slapping Anna's breasts each. Anna took a harsh breath and moaned out loud at the pain and pleasure she received from the slap. She slowly stood with her eyes blindfolded, then turned around to where the order was coming from.

Jacob slowly caressed her two massive breasts, and he brought them closer to his face before roughly grazing his teeth on her hardened nipples. The action made Anna moan hungrily as her body demanded more.

More! More! She wanted to feel more pain and pleasure.

Anna groaned when Jacob pulled her nipple in his mouth and gently sucked on it while grazing his teeth on it too. She moaned out again repeatedly without thinking when she suddenly felt a large arm smashed her ass.

"Ahhh" she groaned when her ass tingled in pain.

She wants more!!

Spreading her thighs, Jackson gave her beautifully rounded ass another spank and watched her fair skin go red from his smashes. Seeing his handprints on her ass, Jackson couldn't help himself from giving her several spanks on her ass, going from gently to roughly in a few minutes.

But no matter how much pain Anna was feeling from it, she welcomed every spank like a good girl. Moaning and groaning softly, the sounds were so enticing to the twins' ears that they couldn't help but lose their composure.

Now everything in their head was to discipline her for being so slutty and making them hard.

Without realizing it, Anna's clothes were immediately shredded off by the twins and the only material on her right now was her bra and the blindfold.

Roughly pushing her to her knees, Jackson dragged Anna's waist and arched her back to position her wet pussy directly on his crotch.

Immediately Jacob saw that she was on her knees, he stood up and dragged down his trousers and his briefs, then his dick sprang free from its captive. Then he suddenly mashed his dick on Anna's face for her to feel how huge, what she was about to take inside her gorgeous mouth was.

Jackson slowly teased Anna's exposed pussy as he trapped her waist and started kneading it on his hardness. Teasing her pussy, as she moaned and she choked on his brother's cock, Jackson couldn't help but give her ass another spank over and over again until he roughly inserted a finger inside her.

Anna couldn't help but gasp out in pleasure at the sudden thrust, "Louder," Jackson commanded as he added another digit. Forcefully spreading her legs apart, Jackson maintained a perfect aggressive rhythm so as not to break her hymen as his fingers started going in and out of her creamy and dripping pussy.

"I said louder, "Jackson commanded again as he pulled his fingers and roughly smacked her ass.

"Ahhhhh, "Anna gasped, choking on Jacob's dick. Her eyes prickled with tears as Jacob wasn't going easy on her either as he held her hair and roughly fucked her mouth with his dick.

She was enjoying every bit of it, she was enjoying how they were making her feel like a sex object. Anna couldn't stop her pussy from releasing more juicy moisture as Jackson kept on fingering her pussy.

The watery and sloppy sound her pussy was making every time he pulled out and inserted his fingers again was enough to make Jackson's dick throb in pleasure.

He quickly removed his fingers and dipped them inside his mouth to taste her juice. Without thinking, he licked his fingers clean. "She tastes so fucking amazing," Jackson announced to his brother when he realized how sweet her pussy juice was.

"I can't wait to have her sit on my face and ride it like a fucking slut, "Jackson added as he immediately pulled off his clothes and released his hardened dick that was already throbbing in excitement.

"Do you want us to remove the blindfold? So, you can see what you are about to take inside your virgin pussy?" Jackson asked as he gently rubbed his dick on Anna's clit.

Assigning to be their sex slave

The slight tension that was slowly building under Anna's region was making her groan, and she slowly trembled before nodding her head.

Yes, she wanted to see.

She wanted to see the dick she had been sucking and also the dick that had been teasing her wet entrance

Jacob slowly untied the blindfold and let Anna's slowly adjust to the vision again until it settled on his dick.

Immediately Anna saw Jacob's dick, her eyes widened in surprise and her pussy tingled in pleasure. She slowly raised her head to look at Jacob who was now totally naked from head to toe.

When Anna raised her gorgeous and innocent eyes at him, Jacob almost lost all reason as he saw the amount of desire in her eyes.

That had to be the most erotic gaze he had ever received since they had been keeping sex slaves.

He doesn't know what was it exactly about their little, shy but wild slave that was making him feel possessive and making his brother wants to fuck her roughly.

"Jackson, the pill." he quickly reminded his brother before he entered her.

They both hated pulling out because they love seeing their slave's pussy oozing out with their cum.

Jackson nodded and went to the drawer that his brother had brought out the blindfold and the cuffs from earlier to get the pills.

Immediately he brought the pill, Jacob went to fetch a glass of water for Anna. Slowly losing the excitement, Anna couldn't help but rub her thigh together in arousal.

They haven't fucked her yet, but she was already wet and dripping with juice from the sexual pleasures.

What was she now? Why did she crave their touch so badly that she couldn't want to be used by them and totally degraded?

It must be the books that Maria always gave her to read, now she totally felt like a slut that her masters have been calling her.

She couldn't believe that her 16 years old sister was also reading books like that.

Waiting for shame and guilt to wash over her, Anna closed her eyes in expectations, but what came over her was another sexual sensation as she felt a large arm on her breast and another finding its way inside her folds. The groans from her masters' voice were sending vibrations to her sensitive areas, and she couldn't help but moan out loud.

The combination of pleasure she felt, as one brother stimulated her erection by rubbing his finger on her clit and the other brother squeezing her breasts, demanded loud moans to break out from her wanton mouth. Sudden sizzling heat started in her, and she couldn't help but shiver under their invasion.

"Please, fuck me," Anna begged like a slut, and they instantly shoved a pill in her mouth and made her swallow it.

"That's for you so you won't get down with a baby, you are married, right? little slave?" Jackson asked when he saw that she had completely swallowed the pill.

This was their usual ritual because they didn't want any of their slaves knocked down with a baby, and started using it to demand money from them after the contract ends.

Anna, who was thinking about how to tell them that they can't Cum inside her, was immediately relieved when they told her what the pill was used for.

"Will you guys fuck me now, please?" She asked innocently, with her eyes filled with intentions of what her body wanted.

Upon hearing her sweet voice and the submission in it, the Mikealsons' brothers groaned heavily and spanked her ass. "This is for you for being naughty, you are not allowed to say anything except how much we are making you feel. You are only allowed to say 'more', You have to tell us you want more of what we are giving you," Jackson declared in a deep aroused voice and slammed his dick inside her wet core.

"Ahhhh, " Anna screamed out because of the pain, and her eyes instantly prickled with tears.

It hurts.

She whimpered as tears flowed down her eyes.

"Be gentle with her, Jackson. You wouldn't want to destroy her newly disvirgined pussy, would you?" Jacob commented when he saw that Anna's eyes were filled with tears.

But Jackson ignored him and voiced out in a commanding tone, "WHAT DID I TELL YOU TO SAY WHEN WE ARE PLEASURING YOU,"

"More, please give me more," Anna screamed out, and Jackson kept fucking her pussy with no mercy. By now, the pain she had felt earlier was gradually turning into pleasure.

When Jacob saw that she wasn't teary as before anymore, he moved closer to her and pinched her nipples with his hands roughly, and Anna winced out again.

"Yes, little slut. The more you scream, the more of this you are going to get, so it's your choice," Jacob said and slowly dragged Anna's upper body up, making her kneel on the couch and forcing her head to wrap against his dick again.

Wrapping her curly hair in his hands, Jacob plunged Anna's head on his dick and roughly filled her mouth while his brother filled her pussy.

"Scream bitch!" Jackson shouted at Anna as he delivered a few strikes to her ass and she immediately let Jacob's dick out of her mouth and screamed with pleasure, "More!! More!l" She screamed out, and she felt her body release another gush of sweet pleasure.

"OhmyGod!" Anna screams out again as waves of pleasure enveloped her whole being.

Every sensible reasoning in Jackson's head immediately went out of the windows when he felt her core tightened around his dick. Thrusting faster and deeper inside her as he spanked her, Jackson shot his cum deep inside her and slowly pulled out when her pussy wrapped around him and milked all his cum.

Immediately after Jackson pulled out, Jacob smiled roughly at Anna, "Spread your legs, let me see your newly disvirgined pussy," He commanded slightly and Anna sat down shyly on the couch again, then spread her legs for the twins to see her pussy which was pink before Jackson invaded her it. Now it looks bruised and thoroughly used.

Slapping her exposed pussy, Jacob smiled evilly at Anna, "Do you like it? Do you like how I feel your throat while my brother was fucking your slutty pussy, ?" He asked, hitting Anna's red and swollen pussy again with his palm.

Anna instantly felt her body accumulating another sexual tension from the vibration of her pussy. The more he slapped her core, the more she screamed out in pleasure.

"See, I told you. She's just perfectly made for us. She looks so much like a sin. I wouldn't mind paying for it." Jacob said to his brother, and Jackson smiled in confirmation.

Definitely, he had no complaints about that. Because his mind immediately jolted back to when he was in that pussy and his dick kept slipping in anytime. He had known that she was made for them, and they aren't letting her go anytime soon.

Jacob was still slapping Anna's pussy and rubbing her clit when a phone started ringing. They looked around and saw that it wasn't their phone, but it was coming from Anna's bag.

They both looked at Anna's expression and instantly knew who was calling, but Jackson still went to retrieve her phone and picked up the phone then gently put it in Anna's ear while his brother continued rubbing her clit.

"Hello," Anna managed to choke out, ignoring the pleasure she was receiving from Jacob's hand.

"Anna, where are you? I just got home," Peter's voice was heard coming from the phone, and she instantly panicked.

Insatiable Anna

That was her husband calling her, she instantly realized when she heard his voice. She instinctively wanted to shrug off Jacob's grab, but he suddenly shoved a finger inside her pussy, and she had to cover her mouth from screaming on the phone with pleasure.

"I. I went to get some stuff from the store, down the street," She managed to lie through her teeth to keep her arousal in check.

Sensing the little discomfort in her voice, Peter kept mute for a while and suddenly asked, "Are you okay?"

"Yeah sure, I'm perfectly okay," She quickly replied then covered her out before another moan escaped her throat.

"Okay, I guess we wouldn't be seeing each other then, since I just came to get a few things, I will be gone in a few minutes. Don't stay out late," Peter asserted and hung up, and Anna suddenly released the pent-up moans she had been holding.

"What is that?" Anna immediately asked after Jacob dropped her gently on the king-sized bed. She saw a golden cage right beside the bed. It was made of gold and it was so huge.

That was when she allowed herself to look around the room, it wasn't a bedroom like her husband's master room because it was filled with different BDSM belts, whips, cuffs, and also something that looks like a big dildo. Anna looked at all the items and felt her body shudder in arousal.

"That is a cage, and this..." Jackson said moving behind Anna's naked body and slowly inhaling the scent in her neck, "is a vibrator," he added, showing her the rabbit-like object.

A vibrator?

What is a vibrator used for? Anna thought innocently, jogging her brain to see if she had read about it before.

As if listening to her thoughts, Jackson used his leg to gently part her thigh and brought the vibrator closer to her clit, and switched on the object.

Anna was still deep in thought when she suddenly felt a zap of electricity rushing down her body, the vibrator was making her clit throb so hard and it was making her wet all over again.

Instead of telling her what it was, Jackson decided to show her what it can do.

He watched her scream and trembled in arousal, and he instantly slammed his dick inside her again roughly as he couldn't control his desires anymore.

Jacob looked at his brother and decided that he would also have to go in that pussy, since his brother seems to like it too much.

"Ahh, yes! More," Anna screamed out when she remembered that they love hearing her say that.

"Fuck, you want more uhn," Jacob asked in a deep voice, moving closer to where Anna was being fucked by his brother in a doggy position.

Seeing her face oozing of pleasure, Jacob's dick instantly got harder, and he groaned in pleasure.

That face!

That face looks so fucking slutty that he wants to slap it so much and made her feel degraded.

"More, please I want more," Anna screamed out in pleasure,

"I could think of "more" to give you, slut," He dragged Anna's face up and smashed his hands over it again and again.

The pain assaulting Anna's head, the pleasure assaulting her core. "Ahhhh, please, please," she pleaded in a low voice.

"Please what? Talk," Jacob asked, attacking her face with another slap while Jackson continued thrusting hard inside her gushing pussy.

Please stop!

Anna wanted to scream out, but she couldn't because she was enjoying it. As painful as the slaps were, she found out that she was also feeling so much pleasure from it.

She was totally confused about whether she wanted them to stop or continue using her as a sex object.

"If you don't talk, I will get angry, and I will punish you," Jacob said as he frowned.

He hates when a slut does not communicate!

Even though they had disvirgined her, she's still a slut to them because that's what she's meant to be.. A slut.

"Please don't stop," Anna whispered incoherently with tears in her eyes.

Did she just say, don't stop? No nooo.

Stop, that was what she wanted to say, but her mouth wasn't even listening to her anymore.

"Oh yess, ahh please" Anna screamed out as she felt her pussy dripping with core and milking Jackson's cock.

She wanted a release, while being demanded, an overwhelming release.

She could already see herself reaching the orgasm, but it was pushed back every time Jackson pulled out his dick or when Jacob stopped slapping her face.

She wanted it all at once. She wanted to be slapped and abused by Jacob while his brother fucked her dirty slutty pussy.

wait, did she just call her pussy a slutty pussy

After a few minutes, Jackson released another load of cum inside Anna's wet pussy and gently picked her up, and put her on the bed.

Anna, who already felt got swollen because of Jackson's dick slightly paled when she thought that he wanted to have sex with her again. She quickly shook her head as she looked at the twins.

"Don't worry, little slut, Daddy won't be fucking you anytime soon again because we had to go out for a while," Jackson said as he slowly moved closer to Anna with a vibrator in his hand.

What did he want to use a vibrator for again? Anna thought, since she knew perfectly well what a vibrator was now.

Did he want to rub it on her clit again?

"Calm down bitch, you are already trembling again. Insatiable aren't you?" Jacob asked as he unlocked the golden cage and smirked at Anna.

She could feel like she was about to be used again, but the twins were acting so strangely for her to understand their next move until Jackson got to the bed and spread her legs open.

"What are you doing?" Anna asked as ripples of pleasure shoot down her spine.

"Why don't you guess, little slut," Jackson replied, gently bending his head and whispering in her ear. "If you guessed right, I might give you another round of sex,"

His deep voice instantly sends havoc down her core and Anna trembles again in desire, "You want to rub it against my clit?" She guessed, but Jackson shook his head and smiled at her.

His smile made him look more like his brother that if she hadn't seen how controlling he was earlier, she would have thought that it was Jacob that was right beside her.

"You guessed wrong!" Jackson answered and instantly shoved the vibrator inside Anna's pussy and watched her quivered in pleasure.

"Uhmmm, ahhhh," Anna moaned out loud, she felt so good. The pulsation she was feeling from the vibrator was sending hot pleasure down her spine, and she couldn't stop herself from moaning.

"How long can you stand that? Did you think you could wait for us with a vibration on your p*ssy?" Jacob asked as he moved closer to Anna and picked her up from the bed.

Anna shivered when she was carried bride-like by Jacob and how he spanked her naked ass. Gently placing her into the golden cage, Jacob brought a timer and set it in front of Anna. "This timer is set for two hours since we should be back by then, but if we are not back before then. You can remove the vibrator after two hours. If you removed it earlier before then, we won't allow you to go home."

Two hours? She's supposed to suffer under this dangerous vibrator for two hours?? Anna instantly shook her head.

She can't, no she can't.

She would orgasm more than 20 times in two hours!

"I can't," Anna mumbled and shook her head as she looked at the twins with tears in her eyes.

She really can't, the pleasure was already building in her belly and she could feel that her orgasm was near.

"If you don't want to go home, You can remove it then." Jackson replied as his brother handed him the lock to the golden cage and instantly looked at it.

"See you later, little slut. Don't miss daddies too much," Jacob said, half smirking at Anna as his eyes looked down at her gushing push again.

When they come back, he will make sure that he fuck that slutty pussy

Jacob, the evil mafia boss

"Do you think she will be able to hold it in before we come back?" Jacob asked, grabbing a blank tailored suit from their wardrobe which was twice a celebrity wardrobe.

"Can't say, she had already received multiple orgasms from us before I inserted the vibrator in her." Jackson replied as he wore his favorite Rolex wristwatch and packed the files they would need in the meeting they were on their way to.

"I hope she holds on though, "Jacob answered, half smirking at his brother.

He was the rascal, as playful and easygoing as he was, he was also the devil that all the little and big mobsters in London feared most. He ran the underground and illegal business of the Mikealsons.

Making him upset was like offending the devil. He didn't forgive nor did he forget!

"Let's talk about the meeting we are going to now, alright?" Jackson answered, he had shifted into the billionaire mood. At this particular meeting, he needed the fireball- who was also his twin brother to hide his usual ways and behave. "I need you to act unconcern till we leave the venue. My secretary added that the man is also running a large mafia house back in the states, so just don't trouble him first, "

"You know I don't trouble them first, " Jacob replied, already feeling hot in the suit he wore. He preferred the casual bad boy clothes, not all these prudish suits that his brother always coerced him to wear anytime they had a meeting to go together.

But no matter how much he hated the suit, he would still put it on because of his brother.

"Yeah, I know you don't." Jackson acknowledged and dialled his driver's phone number.

"We are not spending much time, right?" Jacob asked his brother, following him out of the room.

Even though the two of them were wearing a suit, it completely looked different on Jacob because he flew out both the suit and the inner shirt.

He didn't look a bit like a businessman unlike his brother who had everything in place.

Immediately they walked out of the house, a white Lamborghini stopped slowly and a tall man was seen opening the door of the Lamborghini for his bosses.

"Thank you, Zane," Jackson said to their driver and slowly entered the lambo and watched his town brother fist bump him.

Jackson couldn't help but roll his eyes.

Why did Jacob like scaring Zane so much? He obviously knew that Zane was scared of his fist but he always bumped him.

It wasn't not everything that can withstand your punch brother!

Just get in the car and let's go. He almost shouted at his brother who was playing around when they had a billion pounds deal to secure.

"Jacob, get inside, " Jackson said impatiently to his brother and looked up at Zane to start the car already.

"Okay, okay, let's go get the pounds, " Jacob whistled with a chuckle as he entered the Lambo.

Already bored out of his wit in the car, Jacob tried to video call Anna then he remembered that her phone was in the living room, but she was in the pleasure room.

"Do you think she would have removed the vibrator?" Jacob asked his brother who was surfing the net.

When Jackson heard his question, he thought about it for a while then answered him. "I don't think she will, "

"Really? That would be interesting," Jacob chuckled, a hint of evilness in his voice.

The only thing that made him excited was a naughty slave and guns.

But for now. It was still his Beretta M9 that was his favorite.

Maybe, just maybe she would rise higher. To him, they are both objects that need to be used and pampered.

It wasn't long when they got to CR hotel, it was the second biggest hotel in town. It was second to their company, they would have bought it out if it wasn't owned by a distant cousin their mum cared for, so Jackson advised against it.

Personally, he didn't give a fuck about distant family. The only families he has are his parents and his twin brother. The rest are just members related by blood.

"Hopefully, our new little US mafia will be waiting for us already. Else he would be ruining my mood, "Jacob muttered to his brother as they alighted from the Lamborghini.

"I'm sure, he will be waiting already," Jackson replied, as he walked inside the hotel with confidence. His aura was undeniable, he looked like the reincarnation of an emperor in the mind dynasty. He also looked like Zeus, the king of all of the Greek gods.

The lady at the counter immediately felt her heart skip the instant she saw Jackson. She was memorized. She looked at him with her eyes open, breath stolen. She wasn't able to pull her eyes off his gorgeous face until she heard the door open and another man who was identical to the attractive man before her.

"Close your mouth, Darling. Else you want me to put something in it, " Jacob threw at the receptionist before he flashed their executive cards.

"We have a reservation at the VIP, has someone arrived there already?" Jacob added as he watched the lady's face flushed in pink.

Well, did she have a choice?

That was how they all are. Slutty bitches.

"Uhm, yes sir," The receptionist answered, clearing her throat and the name "Mikealson" flashed In her face.

Were these famous Mikealson brothers?

The angel and the devil? Well not totally Angel and Devil. Just that they were slightly better than each other.

"Okay that's good for him," Jacob dragged out and he gave the receptionist a devilish smirk, "You might need a change of underwear, little slut," He added, in his deep baritone voice and the receptionist instantly felt her pussy clenched in desire.

What the hell!!

That voice... What can that voice do?

The receptionist thought as she watched the Mikealson brothers walk toward the lift.

She felt her pussy drip with juice and softly moaned in pleasure.

Yes, she definitely needs a change of underwear. The secretary thought as she inserted a finger in her pussy and saw how went she was. Now she had to go into the restroom to finish what that devil of a man started.

"You shouldn't joke around in public like that," Jackson scolded his younger twin with a frown.

They hadn't even started the meeting and he was uncontrollable.

"Calm down twin brother, I'm only stating the obvious. I bet she went to the restroom after we left." Jacob replied, pushing the lift button to the first floor but his brother only scowled at him.

"You don't believe me? Should we get the CCTV when we are leaving?" Jacob asked his brother as he flashed his devil smile, then a dimple instantly showed on his perfect cheek.

Vote and comment for a quicker update

Jackson the billionaire

"Stop Joking around, if she's anything it would be 'frightened'. Do you know how you look when you smile like that?" Jackson asked his brother, who didn't seem to have regretted his actions.

It didn't even look like they were bought going to secure a deal, it looked more like Jacob is the uncaring boss and him the serious secretary. "Stop playing around, can we return our attention to the deal we came here for?" He faced his brother with a stern voice, but Jacob only gave one of his usual evil chuckles.

It was the kind of chuckle that if it were his subordinates that saw it, they would have shitted their pants, but because it was Jackson, he only rolled his eyes at his twin brother.

"I'm focused, Brother, I can't wrap my head too seriously around this shit. I will feel like it's blowing." Jacob confessed, half jokingly. He really hated all these official meetings, board meeting anything that had to do with him acting grim and serious, he just fucking hates it.

He prefers his part of the business that deals with drug trafficking, building BDSM clubs, prostitutes, illegal ammunition, and so on.

He is a lion, he can't be locked in a cage called an office.

"Hello, Sirs. Welcome to our VIP section. Do you have a reservation?" A pretty brunette greeted with a smile immediately she spotted two handsome men coming to the counter in suits. They both looked handsome, exuding the aura of an emperor and a general, and it's making her head spin.

She was so ecstatic that she helped her colleague with her shift because she would have regretted it so much her entire life if she hadn't seen these two gods today.

Upon hearing her voice, Jackson and Jacob brought out their cards and asked for directions.

"Just down the hall," The pretty brunette answered, dipping her voice a little lower to sound seductive, also making sure that her blouse strap was falling off her shoulder when she saw the name written on their cards.

THEY ARE THE MIKEALSON BROTHERS!!

Her eyes almost popped out of its socket, she didn't expect them to look this good-looking and extraordinary in reality.

She had seen them in different newspapers, Instagram, even on Pinterest. Because their pictures always featured "Hottest man alive" in the tags.

Jackson and Jacob were about to the counter when a brawny, short-haired man saw them, and Jackson instantly remembered his face as the man who they were signing the deal with.

"Mr. Frank?" Jackson asked, and the man turned around to look at who called his name.

Shocked, he called out, "Mr. Mikealson? You are here,"

"I just got here, can you lead us to the seat please?" Jackson asked politely. That was when Mr. Frank saw that he wasn't alone. Did he bring a mirror with him? Mr. Frank thought as he turned around to see a replica of Jackson.

But the dressing instantly told him that it was not a mirror, but Mr. Jackson's rebellious twin brother.

Why is he even here? He frowned when he saw that Jacob was totally ignoring him as if he didn't exist. Or as if he weren't in his presence.

His mood instantly dampened but then it wasn't Jacob's fault either, he just can't be bothered to greet people that's less than him, especially not a little mafia gang from the trenches of the United States.

He didn't even know why they had to go for these deals. He is a dope peddler and arms dealer, all this office shit got nothing on him.

When Jackson saw that they weren't going to end the staring contest anytime soon, he cleared his throat, and it instantly brought Mr. Frank back to his senses and he quickly gave an awkward smile and led them to the reserved seat.

Immediately they got seated, Jackson brought out the documents and spread them out for Mr. Frank to go over them again.

"I've already gone through it some minutes before you got here, your secretary sent them to my mail, she said you might be late. You were. " Mr. Frank retorted, giving Jackson a brief look. He was so angry that he felt like he could burst when he saw the message, and it was exactly what the secretary said. He really did arrive late.

Had it been he was in the states, he would have canceled the goddamn deal and also run their asses down.

"Oh, she said that?" Jackson asked, looking suspiciously at his brother, and slowly raised his eyebrows at him.

"Yeah, I asked her to say that. So, he can keep himself occupied while he waits, " Jacob answered his brother with a shrug, clearly not seeing the sin he committed.

Jackson gently rubbed his temple in frustration and exhaustion. He was asking him to not make trouble when they left the mansion, not knowing that he had already made trouble.

And he still had the cheek to say it out loud.

Keep himself occupied, the hell!

"Jacob," He dragged out in caution when he saw Mr. Frank's ugly, angry face.

"What?"Jacob answered ignorantly before he turned his attention to Mr. Frank, then saw that he was delaying the deal. "Since he had already read the contract, what is he still waiting for?" He asked his brother as if the 'He' he was talking about wasn't in front of him.

Unable to take the utter disrespect anymore, Mr. Frank ranted out, "Mr. Mikaelson, is this how you do business? Bringing your brother who isn't in the system to ruin a billionaire deal?"

"Isn't it just a Billion?"Jacob scoffed under his breath, but it was audible enough for Mr. Frank to hear.

Jackson held his temple again and heavily breathed down before taking control of the situation because he knew if it continued like this, Mr. Frank or plank would not sign the deal with them anymore.

"Mr. Frank. I don't think my brother is totally wrong. What he did was actually of your interest because if you had sat down and waited for us for a few minutes without doing anything, and we had to start going through the documents again before signing, it would be another waste of time. And what we businessmen don't have much is time.., isn't it, Mr. Frank?" Jackson rephrased what his twin brother had said in a more gentleman and businessman-like way.

"Sure," Mr. Frank, who couldn't see that it was still the same words, smiled slowly.

It was still Jackson Michelson that was the best to deal with and not his devilish brother.

He better watch out whenever he comes to the states because he already has his eyes on him.

"Jackson, didn't you tell him that I don't like when people stare at him?" Jacob asked his brother when he saw that Mr. Frank kept on throwing glances at him, and it was frustrating.

The only people that can look at him that much are girls that he wanted to possess and make his sex slave. Like little Anna- oh damn is it not almost 2 hours already?

"Are we going to sign the goddamn deal or not, did he not have better things to do?" Jacob added impatiently.

The Baby mafia king of the States is delaying his precious time. They still had to go back home and fulfilled all their little sex slave fantasies, but he was just glancing at him as if he had two heads.

"Mr. Frank, I think we should close the deal already," Jackson asserted, seeing that his twin brother is now getting impatient.

And if Jacob is impatient, he gets uncomfortable and furious. He doesn't want another round of fights and most especially because they don't have all day since a lovely little girl is waiting for them to remove the vibrator in her pussy.

"Sure," Mr. Frank answered and quickly brought out a fountain pen and drew his signature on the documents.

"Nice doing business with you," Mr. Frank said, stretching his hand after retrieving his copy of the document and Jackson replied as he shook his outstretched hand with a smile plated on his face.

"Same here," Jackson replied, and Jacob instantly stood up from the chair and left.

He doesn't like Mr. Frank's face, and he doesn't feel looking at him more than necessary, as he couldn't find any reasons to stay in his presence any longer.

"Goodbye, " Jackson said to Mr. Frank before walking in large strides to meet his brother.

"You couldn't even leave a comment, you just left the meeting so abruptly, " Jackson retorted, catching up with his brother.

"Thought the deal is closed already, " Jacob muttered and brought out his phone to search for new nightgowns for their little slut to wear since she might not be leaving anytime soon.

During the meeting, he couldn't even imagine her dripping pussy in peace as Mr. Frank or whatever his name was kept intruding on his daydreams with his ugly bald head.

"Do you think Anna would like this?" Jacob said to his brother as he showed him a pink lace nightgown that almost looked like gothic clothing.

Jackson looked at the image and couldn't help but think about Anna, because for a girl like Anna who had worn a matching bra and panties, she must definitely like a more childish pajamas instead of a sexy nightgown but he knew that his brother wouldn't consider that option at all.

"How about we go to a store and get all this for her?" Jacob asked his brother again when he saw that he hasn't answered his last question

Maybe he couldn't choose.

"You know we can order this online, yeah? " Jackson asked, he was so tired and exhausted he needed a little nap. So he can perfectly pleasure the little bitch that was waiting for them.

"Yeah, I know, " Jacob answered but he still stubbornly refuses to order online. When Zane saw his bosses approaching he quickly drove the Lamborghini to where they were and they left the hotel premises.

"So are we going home now?" Jackson asked Jacob, but the man he was asking a question was busy viewing sexy nightgowns for their sex slave.

"No, to the store, " Jacob replies in a firm voice, but he didn't look away from his phone.

Y'all not gonna leave your comments? *Heartbroken*

Nightgown for their new slave?

When Jackson knew that there was nothing he could do to change his brother's mind, he decided to just get on with it.

It wasn't that he wasn't interested in picking nightgowns for their new slave, it was just that it was unusual for them to do so, and Jacob was taking it seriously as if he was going to select guns for his Mafia gang.

"That one is very pretty, " Jackson pointed out, looking at the nightgown on Jacob's phone that read VEJARO lace Sexy lingerie. He liked how short the nightgown was and also how it cupped the dummy body.

"Really? It's good, yeah? I was also thinking the same thing, " Jacob replied, flashing his brother a contagious grin that made Jackson also smile.

Sometimes his brother looks so innocent that people wouldn't know how maniacal he was unless he spoke, or flashed his devilish grin. It was mostly the devilish grin that always exposed his vicious aura and attitude because he rarely talked except when the person was a beautiful girl, or when he gave orders to his subordinate.

"Yes, let's get that and a couple more like it, " Jackson answered with a smile again.

Even though they were identical, they had different likes and dislikes except when it comes to females because they always have the same female at the same time. They've never had a girlfriend because they don't know how to court. They only knew how to make a female get down on her knees and accept that they were her daddies and masters nothing more.

That was how it has always been, and that's how it will always be.

"Can we grab some ice cream too, " Jackson asked when he suddenly felt an urge to taste something sweet and melty in his mouth.

"Yeah, sure. I'd like some too, " Jacob answered, but Jackson's mind was already on something else that was tasty and melty in his mouth.

Anna's juicy cum.

It was so tasty and melty when he tasted it, he had wanted to get down and spread her legs apart, so as to let her dripping juice flow directly in his mouth, but he knew that if he had done so, they would be later than necessary for the meeting and it was kind of important.

After a few minutes, Zane pulled up in front of a huge lingerie boutique, and the two brothers gracefully got out of the car.. This time they had put on glasses and a mask, so that they wouldn't be recognized by anyone.

Jackson had suggested it with a quote that he wouldn't be caught dead in a lingerie boutique and Jacob had agreed because he felt his brother already did a lot tonight.

When they got inside the boutique, they were still ogled by the ladies who were inside the boutique shopping. Because it was stated clearly on the board that it was a "Ladies Lingerie boutique" and they could still see two tall and handsome men inside acting like a natural like what the hell are they doing here?

"Do you think they came to get lingeries for their girlfriends?" A lady in the boutique section asked her friend who had tagged along just because she had promised to get her one.

"Probably, but look at the suit they are putting on, doesn't that look like a TOM FORD suit?" Her friend replied after she carefully looked at the two men, she might not know anything about these two men but she can say that they are extremely wealthy and she would love to have a conversation with them. Who knows, she might be lucky and ask her out.

But they are probably in a relationship, a tiny voice said in her head, but she ignored it.

Well, they didn't necessarily have to be in a relationship at this age to get lingerie for a girl yeah? The girl thought, and with that thought, she loose guarded her friend who had promised her lingerie and went after the hot men.

"Hello, is there a particular lingerie you are searching for?"

Jackson and Jacob heard a voice from their back and instantly turned around to see a girl flashing a smile at them.

"Are you a sales attendant?" Jacob asked curiously in his deep normal voice, totally interested in getting what was on his mind, but the girl smiled and scratched her neck awkwardly.

"Uhm, No. I'm not an employee here. I just wanna help out," She replied and Jackson instantly frowned. He wasn't expecting any audience and he didn't even expect anyone to approach them. If he had known that his brother would be so interested in getting lingerie, he would have booked the goddamn boutique ahead.

"Don't worry we got-

Jackson was about to kindly decline the lady's kind offer but Jacob interrupted him, "Sure, we got some stuff we'd like to buy. Can you show us where to get this," Jacob said, then showed her the pictures of lingeries he had marked 'favorite' on his phone.

"Oh, Uhm. Ah . Alright," She instantly flushed pink when she saw the lingeries pictures. "Are these for your girlfriends? What are their sizes?" She added, feeling her body tingling with desire.

She wished she was one of the girls that would be putting this on. She thought when she remembered how sexy the lingerie on the man's phone was.

But unknowingly to her, all the lingeries belong to just one girl.

Jacob looked at his brother at the mention of a girlfriend and Jackson immediately shook his head.

No, what the hell.

"Uhm, it's uhmm.. a present for a friend," Jacob let out and the girl instantly flashed a smile that can be interpreted as a seductive smile.

"What about her size? Do you have an idea?" She asked again, this time she had dropped her voice a little bit and it can be told that she was entirely faking it, but Jacob already had his devilish smile and Jackson knew that he had found a new plaything.

Jackson looked at her with pity in his eyes, she probably wouldn't know that his vicious brother had turned her into an amusing doll. Well, it's her fault for poke nosing.

"What do you think her size could be?" Jacob asked his brother as he imagined Anna's body, but he couldn't efficiently think about her size because he could only imagine her naked and looking at him with her soulful brown eyes.

But Jackson, who did a better job in remembering her size, informed the lady and she led them to get lingerie of that particular size.

Her friend who she had loose guarded was utterly speechless, she could only stare at her and the two handsome men retreating back as they went into another section.

When did Cynthia turn into a sales attendant? And she even discarded her as if she wasn't the one that brought her into the boutique in the first place.

She just can't believe what she was witnessing, fine. She would just leave her alone. Let her find her way to the hostel herself. She muttered to herself and paid for the stuff she had bought, then left the boutique.

The cashier didn't even ask about her friend since she could also see how she had ditched her, so she just focused on her business until she came outside again with the two men, pushing a cart full of lingerie as she talked to them.

If one didn't know, they would think that she had arrived with the men, but the cashier had seen her come with her friend so she felt disgusted that a lady could bring herself as low as this just because the men were handsome and they were wearing very expensive suits.

"Can you please calculate this?" Jackson asked the cashier, gently shoving the lady to a side making sure that she didn't touch anything that belongs to their slave. But the lady was extremely happy because her body had come in contact with his body and she felt goosebumps all over her body.

Jacob looked at her and smiled wickedly, he actually didn't mind her shameless act. Infact, he kinda liked shameless girls because they would be easy to use and abuse as they were already shameless. He wouldn't have minded too much if Anna wasn't waiting in their house with a vibrator in her pussy.

"5000 pounds sir, " The cashier answered after carefully calculating all the lingeries, and the girl instantly felt her head spinning.

She knew that everything the men had picked would be expensive but she didn't expect it to be more than 3000 pounds but the cashier just said that everything was 5000.

Holyfuck! She must definitely go home with them. She said to herself determinedly.

"Alright, " Jackson brought out his debit card and paid for all the lingerie, then the cashier packed everything and smiled at them before her gaze dropped to the lady beside them with scorn.

Shameless! She muttered but the lady only looked away and ignored her.

Just wait, till she had one of these men to her, she would make sure that she brought him here to get all their lingeries.

When they got outside the boutique, Zane immediately alighted from the Lamborghini to get the bags from his bosses but they waved him off since everything in the bags belong to their sex and they don't want anyone touching it.

When Cynthia saw someone coming out of a Lamborghini and towards them, her eyes almost came out of its socket.

Who the hell are these men?

They even got a Lambo!

No!!! She must definitely go with -

"Thank you, Ma'am, for your kind behavior but we have to go now, " Jackson interrupted her thought since he knew that he can't let his brother end it since Jacob's mouth doesn't have a filter. He brought out some paper denominations from his wallet and gave them to the lady for her kindness and instantly left for the Lambo but Jacob still stayed a bit and winked at the lady.

So boring, he thought. His brother just doesn't know how to catch fun.

He was thinking of taking the girl home and letting her see how they fuck Anna after they put the lingerie on her, so she can imagine herself in Anna's shoes, but Jackson spoiled his plan.

He reluctantly went after his brother and Zane instantly drove back to the mansion.

"Do you think we stayed too long?" Jacob asked his brother immediately after they alighted the car.

Check the book rank out

Do you miss us, little slut?

"Yeah, we actually stayed too long, and that was because you decided to start flirting with a hooker, " Jackson answered, staring at his brother with a frown, but Jacob only smiled his usual vicious smile which did not affect his twin brother in any way since he was used to it.

When they got to the sitting room, they saw Anna's phone and discovered that she had several missed calls from a contact saved as "Husband" and Jackson instantly frowned.

Why is he calling her that much? He furrowed his brows, forgetting that they were the one the girl was cheating with.

Jacob left his brother in the sitting room and went inside the pleasure room to get on Anna. immediately he got there, he was instantly speechless.

Anna was cuddled up in the golden cage, with the vibrator dripping with cum out of her and sound asleep. She looked like the sexy version of sleeping beauty with her lips slightly apart and her soft slow breaths.

Jacob was looking at her, totally taken in with the image before him when his brother came inside, he saw him standing mouth open and staring at Anna.

"She's pretty, Yeah?" Jackson asked, and after a while, Jacob nodded in confirmation.

"Yeah, she's so fucking pretty, " he answered as took the key out to unlocked the golden cage, then gently picked Anna up and carried her into the bathtub.

"Are you gonna bathe her?" Jackson asked shocked, as he followed him into the bathroom where he had placed Anna and he was now looking for a bath soap, but she was still fast asleep.

Jacob really wanted to bath a girl? Like he actually wanted to bath their slave?

"Sure, why not. She has cum all over her, " Jacob replied as if he was doing the most natural thing in the world, but even he knew that he was going out of bound. He just felt her doing this at the moment, and it felt so damn right to him.

When he saw that his brother really meant business, Jackson went to get a towel and gave it to his brother so he could wrap Anna with it when he was done.

Startled, Anna instantly woke up when she felt her body drowning in water and quickly fluttered her eyes open. She looked up to see Jacob with a half smirk on his face gently rubbing some soap on her body and she instantly shivered.

He was bathing her!

Why was he bathing her?? Her brain instantly exploded when she finally processed the information.

"Jacob, why-"

"Shh, just lie down and let daddy bathe you, Okay?" Jacob interrupted her speech and Anna looked up to see Jackson beside the door winking at her.

Everything felt so unreal, wasn't she in the cage waiting for them to come earlier?

When did they arrive? And how did she get into the bathtub?

"When did you guys arrived?" Anna slowly asked after a while when Jacob was slowly rubbing the soap behind on her shoulders and slowly massaging it.

She never knew that a bath could be so sensual and could make her remember how her pussy was dripping so hard from the effect of the vibrator they had inserted in it before they left for their meeting.

At first, she had wanted to remove the vibrator after an hour when they left, but she remembered Jacob's promise and decided to hold on until they came back until she fell asleep.

"We came back so minutes ago, you were asleep and you were dripping with so much juice, " Jackson answered from the door in a deep voice as if he was imagining the scene again in his head and Anna's cheek flushed pink and her body instantly shivered again.

She was such a slut for these two men. She literally just met them but she's so attracted to them that her body got turned on even with a smile from them.

"Look at you getting all horny again, aren't you tired little vixen?" Jacob asked, rubbing the soap slowly on her neck and moving deliberately to her breasts. A smile hung in his lip as his soapy hands wrapped around them, and he squeeze them softly.

Anna raised her big soulful eyes at Jacob and slowly moaned out from the pressure Jacob was applying on her breast. "Continue looking at me like that, and this bath won't be a successful one." Jacob threatened when Anna gently bit on her lips and dragged it with her teeth.

Fuck!

Jacob felt his groin explode, he directly brought her bitten lips closer to him and sucked on them roughly, and watched it go from pink to red in an instant.

Anna's vision instantly blurred with passion, and she couldn't stop herself from leaning closer to Jacob to feel more of his lips and let him run his tongue inside her mouth. She moaned in pleasure because she had never felt this good. Her first kiss wasn't like this, she had almost thought that kiss was meant to be like the brief and unattractive one that her husband gave her when they had signed their impromptu marriage, but Jacob was giving her another insight into what a real kiss is and she was enjoying every bit of it.

She pressed her wet body closer to his chest, totally unaware that he was still putting on his expensive suit. Anna slowly dragged her hands inside the suit and clenched on Jacob's abs grazing her fingers on his hard chest as she licked her lips again.

"I think she really missed us, " Jackson said to his brother, gently pulling off his clothes. Leaving only his trousers on as she moved closer to his brother and Anna.

"Really, is that true? Do you miss us little slut?" Jacob asked as he brought out Anna's hands under his chest, and slowly washed it with the soap in his hand. He didn't care about his expensive suit, the only thing that mattered right now to him was the little pretty sex kitten in front of him.

Totally sad about the disconnect of her hands on his chest, Anna felt disappointed and muttered slowly. "Yes,"

Jackson gave a throaty chuckle as he switched the tap, and Anna's soapy body was instantly cleansed. The bath was cut short.

He couldn't wait anymore. He doesn't know what exactly it is about Anna that makes him impatient.

All inhibitions are gone, he retrieved the towel from his brother and draped it around Anna's body, and carried her outside of the bathroom. This time, they didn't take her into the sitting room or the pleasure room. They took her into their master room and gently placed her on the king-sized bed.

Anna was speechless at the gentle way they were treating her but her heart was beating fast and warming up to it that she had to constantly remind herself that she's a married woman and this is just a fling.

It's a fling! It's a fling, she continues reminding herself.

Wrapped in a towel and seated on the bed, Anna watched as Jacob brought some stuff with him and gently placed them beside her.

"What are these?" she asked curiously as it was wrapped and she couldn't see it.

"It's nightgowns, Jacob was suddenly interested in getting you some. That was the reason why we were later and expected, " Jackson answered and threw his brother a gaze but Jacob just shrugged his shoulders and picked his favorite pack from the collection and store it open, revealing a lace red lingerie. Moving closer to Anna with his usual half smirk on his face, his eyes focused on her trembling red lips and he remembered how he had bitten it so hard a few minutes ago and his dick tightened immediately.

No, they can't go inside her right now. No matter how delicious and sexy she was looking right now.

He had to refrain himself from touching her, or else he won't be able to control his unexplainable sexual urges. "Can you put this on?" Jacob asked, giving up the thought of wearing it for her since he wanted to hold the reins of his desire.

"Okay, " Anna answered slowly and took the lace lingerie for him.

This is the first time she would be getting lingerie from a man and it wasn't even her husband.

It was some men she had met online on a dating platform and had decided to visit, thinking that she would go back home the same day but here she was wearing the lingerie they took their time to buy for her after she had been used and fucked by them.

If someone had told her yesterday or the day before that she would be in some men's house, on her knees and letting them fill her virgin holes with their dicks, she would have sworn to her abusive father that it can never happen.

But it did!

She actually cheated on her new husband with some strangers with very good dicks, and she still wanted more. The hunger in her hadn't reduced a bit even with the vibrator and the several orgasms that they had given her before they left.

She still wanted them to fill her holes at the same time and make her climax heavily.

"What are you thinking of?" Jacob asked when he saw that Anna was looking at him dazed.

Is she thinking about her useless husband?

More Ice cream or another cream?

"Uhn?" Anna asked, blinking her eyes as she came out of her daydream.

"He said, what are you thinking of?" Jackson replied, looking up at Anna's flushed cheeks and he instantly became interested in what she was thinking of too.

It better not be something he wouldn't like to hear.

For example, her husband.

He doesn't even want to think about it again even when it was the first thing that attracted him to her. The thought of fucking her and making her admit that she was cheating was the first thing that made him started fantasing about her.

"I..uhmm.. I was thinking about about about.." Anna stuttered, looking at the two brothers innocently. She didn't know how to tell them that she had been thinking about their dicks and how much she wanted it.

"Since you don't want to talk about it, keep it yourself. But you have to stop thinking. We want your body and soul here. Not some other places, " Jacob declared in a deep voice when he saw that she couldn't say a proper sentence.

It was that moment that Jackson remembered that they had gotten some ice creams on their way back home. "Do you want some ice cream?" He asked.

At the thought of eating some ice cream, Anna flashed a childish smile at Jackson and nodded her head in excitement. It has been forever since she had eaten ice cream.

If she could remember currently, it was some months before her mother died and that was two years ago.

Since then her life had turn upside down, and she had became another person in her body shell.

"You like ice cream?" Jacob asked, when she saw her childish expression and instantly chuckled. Her expression right now looked like a five years old girl and it made him want to ruffle her curls.

"Yes, " Anna answered, flushing pink in embarrassment. She didn't know that her enthusiasm for eating ice cream was written on her face. She felt like burying herself under the duvet.

"I'm gonna go get them, " Jackson let out and briefly left the room.

"Why are you so excited about eating ice cream? " Jacob asked, sitting beside Anna on the bed. Looking a the her flushed cheeks with a half smirk.

He could look at her all day. Why was she so fucking beautiful? Looking at her closely now, she could see that she had little freckles dusted on her cheeks.

"Because it has been so long, more than two years ago," Anna muttered in a low price and looked away in sadness. She didn't want to remember anything tonight.

She just wanted to forget her worries and sorrows and let her body welcome the two men that have been pleasuring her.

Seeing her expression, Jacob understood that it was a personal thing and decided to drop the conservation. It was at that time that Jackson came inside with a huge container of ice cream and gently placed it on the bed, and gave Anna and Jacob a spoon each.

Looking excitedly at the ice cream, Anna couldn't wait for the vanilla ice cream with strawberry toppings to make in her mouth.

How did they know her favorite?

Jacob and his brother hadn't even taken more than two spoons each, when they saw that Anna had already eagerly eaten her part of the ice cream and she was already moving to theirs.

It didn't take up to 10 minutes, Anna already gulped the ice cream and was now gently licking her lips with her tongue and the twins were staring at her as if she had grown two heads, "What?" Anna asked, licking her thumb as she stared at them with her big brown eyes.

"You ate it all?" They let out in sync and Anna nodded her head, with a sheep smile.

At that moment, she looked so much like a child that the twins felt the urge to properly own her and pamper her.

"Do you want more?" Jacob asked, edging closer to her and gently patted her head with a devious smile on his face. Anna who didn't know that the smile means trouble nodded,

"Can I get more?"

"Say it properly, like a little slut." Jacob demanded grabbing her cheeks and squeezing her face. Making her look at him as if her next breath depends on him.

"Please, can I have more ice cream, " She let out a soft moan.

Why did she always feel horny when they talk dirty to her? How did a single demand for ice cream make her think it wasn't the same ice cream that she had eaten that he was talking about.

"Jacob, I think you need to clarify what kind of ice cream you are talking about because our little slut here is already thinking about something else," Jackson told him and Jacob laughed out loud.

"Is that true Anna? Are you thinking about another ice cream? Or do you want the one you just finished eating?" Jacob asked in a deep provocation voice, at the moment he sounded like a maniac, and Anna couldn't help but shiver.

Why did she like it when he talked to her like that?

Instantly, she didn't know whether she wanted an ice cream or another cream deep in her mouth.

"I...uhmm. " She stuttered as she looked at them with her eyes full of uncontrollable desire. Clearly, she was losing a battle of choice because her stomach wanted more ice cream but her wanton and slutty body wanted another cream.

She was torn in between saying she wanted ice cream or she wanted their cream inside her.

"Jacob, Let's get the poor girl more ice cream. I don't think she can handle us if we start with her again. With how she wolfed down the ice cream, I think she's really hungry, " He reminded his brother and stood up to get a big coat for Anna to wear over her nightgown.

"Yeah, sure. Let's go get more ice creams and some steaks, " Jacob nodded to his brother. He's really craving steaks. The grilled steaks, those per grilled ones that always almost taste raw.

"What is the coat for?" Anna asked when she saw Jackson coming towards her with a big black coat.

Aren't they going out to get the ice cream? Or wait.. Are they taking her with them?

"For you to wear love, do you think we are going to leave you here again?" Jacob answered Anna's question and gently cupped her breast and squeezed it unhurriedly. He really loves seeing her in this nightgown so much that he doesn't even want to go out. He would have let her go with them in this nightgown but he doesn't want anyone apart from him and his brother to see her like this.

But her husband will... A tiny voice reminded Jacob and he instantly frowned. Guess they would have to do something about that.

"I'm coming along?" Anna asked bewildered, aren't they scared of going out with her? What if her husband sees her? She didn't know much about her husband but she knew that he's a very mysterious person and he has a cold glare that makes her think that he's not that simple.

"Sure, don't you want to?" Jacob asked with a frown. He hates when sluts are not comparative.

"I can't go with you guys, what if someone sees me with you? I'm a married woman, " Anna said slowly and dipped her head down.

"If I say you are going, then you are going with us," Jackson replied and threw the coat on the bed and left the room in anger. Slamming the door hand as he left.

He hates when she brings up the fact that she's a married woman. He hates thinking that she belongs to another man.

"Is he angry?" Anna asked Jacob who was still beside her but Jacob was still staring at the door in disbelief. Did his calm and collected brother just act on his feelings? Isn't he always uncaring and pattern minded?

He knew for certain that it was because their pretty little slut mentioned the word "husband" that was why his brother was so angry.

Wasn't he the one that was supposed to be reminding them that she's a married woman?

"Yeah, he's angry and did you know what I told you that he will do when he's angry?" Jacob said in his deep voice to Anna.

Upon hearing his voice, Anna's mind instantly became muddled, "He will punish me?" She asked blinking her glossy eyes because it was dark, the action looked so seductive to Jacob that he felt desire rushing down his groins. Why did she have to be so security and innocent?

It makes him want to dominate her as he had dominated the whole of western states apart from the United States. Which will also be soonest when all his plans are fully achieved. All the western states will belong to the Michelson'.

"Yes, Little slut, You have to go with us else he will really punish you and I won't be able to save you from his deep and everlasting thrusts, so tell me. Are you coming with us or not?" Jacob asked, cocking an evil smile at Anna.

Teasing Anna in the Ice cream store.

Anna couldn't stop her body from trembling when she heard Jacob say 'deep and everlasting thrusts'. She would have refused to go because of that, but she also knew that she was very hungry and she needed to eat.

"Fine, I will go with you guys," Anna finally decided and wore the big black coat on her nightgown. She didn't know how ridiculously pretty and little she looked inside the coat because of her figure until she saw herself in a mirror on their way out of the mansion.

She instantly wanted to go back and wore the clothes she was putting on when she came in the morning, but she heard Jackson's voice, "If you go back inside, I will assume that you don't need the ice cream anymore and you wanted to be fucked instead. So think carefully before you take your next step,"

Meanwhile, Jacob left to bring his car which was also one of his toys, "You guys coming in?" He asked from the car and Jackson nodded then opened the door for Anna to get inside. Leaving her with no choice but to go out to the Ice cream store.

It wasn't long when Jacob pulled up in front of an ice cream store. Anna looked up and saw "Amirrino" written boldly on the front door of the ice cream store and she could also see so many people inside the ice cream store.

She suddenly didn't want to get out of the car, she didn't like seeing people. Can't they just go and get the ice cream and bring it back inside the car?

Since her father made her stop her education and turned her into a maid while abusing and maltreating her, she had grown a social phobia and she wasn't confident in showing herself to the public.

"Don't you want to go out?" Jacob asked, peering at her from the side mirror when he saw her long look at the ice cream store. "Jackson, can you book the whole goddamn ice cream store for the next three hours? I think our little slut here doesn't like seeing other people. And I kinda like that idea," he added when he saw Anna flinch at his question.

A whole store with them and their little slut alone, hmm. That does really bring lots of ideas in his head and he couldn't wait to start executing them.

"Sure, " Jackson replied and dialed his Secretary number to book the ice cream store.

Linda, who was already dozing off after she finished drafting her boss's schedule, was instantly jolted awake by the sound of her ringtone.

It was her boss, she was able to identify who was calling even before she picked up the phone because she had personalized a different ringtone for her boss contact.

One of the things her boss hated most was when his call was delayed or he couldn't get through. Clearing her throat and washing the dizziness of her face she picked the call. "Hello sir," she answered as waited for her boss' deep and cold voice to respond back to her.

"Hello Linda, can you book Amirrino Ice cream store for 3 hours?" Jackson asked, directly when he saw that the call was connected.

Uhn? Amirrino? Don't tell me he called her late in the night around 9 pm to ask her to book an ice cream store?

No! No one told her that this was part of her job description when she interviewed for the job of a Secretary in the Michealson's company.

"Sir?" She asked again, trying to verify that he actually asked her to book an ice cream store.

And what is her boss doing in an ice cream store for crying out loud? But be that his Devil handsome twin brother because her boss would have gone for wine instead of an ice cream.

So she was sure that it must be his devilish twin that brought the ridiculous idea.

"Do I have to repeat myself?" Jackson asked in a grim voice. He didn't have all the time, Anna is hungry and they still have to go back to pleasure her and make her feel dirty. So he doesn't have time to be repeating himself over a single order.

"No no no sir, you don't. I got it. Booked Amirrino for three hours. I will get back to you in 5 minutes?" Linda quickly answered because she knew that her boss might get angry and tell her to resign.

"Okay, five minutes." Jackson retorted and hung up.

Anna who didn't know what was happening, since she was lost earlier couldn't help but stare at Jackson in shock when she heard him call someone and told him/her to book the store.

She looked back at the ice cream store and saw how massive it was, it must definitely be overly expensive.

She knew that they were rich because of their big mansion and how prosperous and beautiful the designs were, but she didn't know that they were wealthy enough to really book the ice cream store.

After five minutes, Linda called back. "Hello Sir, I've booked the whole Amirrino and it would be available between now and the next 15 minutes, they offered their apologies that it can't be as sooner than this,"

"Anna, can you wait for 15 more minutes?" Jackson asked while he was on the call with Linda.

"Yeah, it's fine. I can wait, " Anna answered in a low voice. Still not believing that they were really booking up the whole Amirrino just because she couldn't go out to eat.

After her reply, Jackson went back on his call and told Linda that it was okay and they would wait for the next 15minutes. She was instantly bewildered and dazzled.

And who was Anna?

She hasn't heard her boss bring up or say anything about someone named "Anna" before? Is she their new pet? Linda thought after her boss dropped the call.

"Since we have 15 minutes to ourselves, what did you think we should do?" Jacob asked, after coming out of the car to sit beside Anna, sandwiching her between them.

It was when Anna heard Jacob's deep voice that she understood what was going on. She was now inside the twin's entrapment again.

"I didn't think of that, " Jackson replied, entirely commending his brother's decision with a smile. Leave it to Jacob to bring out a favorable action out of an unfavorable one.

With this talent of his, if he had been interested in the business world instead of the mafia world, he would have been an iconic and chronic business lord.

Anna looked at them innocently as she prepared for what was coming, she didn't know if she would be able to accept any of their dicks inside her right now as she was still a bit swollen from Jackson's penetration earlier since she was just disvirgined.

She slightly shivered, when she felt Jacob's hot breath on her neck. She wriggled her back and arched closer to him and Jacob read her perfectly.

Such a little slutty bitch. Since she wanted it so much then he will give it to her.

His experienced hands immediately went under Anna's waist and lifted her up. Firmly positioning her in between his dick, he slowly opened the buttons of the black coat that Anna was putting on and revealed the red lace lingerie she was having under.

Yes, he likes this red lingerie she was putting on. If he knew that it would have this much effect on him, he would have bought more like it when the little hooker was flirting and rubbing her breasts all over him and his brother.

Gently pulling off the coat, Jackson watched Anna's naked breasts from the side and instantly felt horny. He watched as Jacob's hands found her enormous breasts and rubbed them roughly after pinching her nipples. Anna could feel her nipples get hard. Looking at her hardened nipples, Jacob couldn't help but rip the red lace lingerie open without warning. Exposing her breasts and hardened nipples for his and his brother's naked eyes.

Anna automatically felt her pussy clenched in pleasure when she saw the hunger in their eyes.

Are they going to fuck her in the car? Today is the first time she would be having sex and she already wanted to experience car sex? Her body trembled in anticipation when she imagined their dicks going through her holes.

Jacob was ogling at Anna's breasts and was about to bring her tits in his mouth when he felt some wetness on his trousers. He gently lifted her up from his lap and saw that her pussy was dripping and it had wet his trousers.

Damn! Their little slut is really a naughty whore. She's always wet and horny for their cocks.

"Damn, she's really dripping, " Jackson said as his fingers found their way to Anna to stroke her wet dripping cunt.

"Why are you so wet? Are you expecting my brother's dick inside you that soon? Aren't you ashamed that we are outside in public?" Jackson asked before he pushed a finger inside Anna's pussy.

You still have the vibrator on?

Anna's eyes closed briefly at the sudden intrusion and she breathed heavily. She definitely wasn't expecting him to do that.

"You don't have to be shy, Anna, answer my question," Jackson urged.

When he saw that she wasn't still replying, he brought out the vibrator he had remembered to bring with him and inserted it into her wet core.

Jacob, who was watching their actions all this while in amusement, looked out of the car and saw that the customers in the ice cream store were leaving one after the other. "I think it's about time we go get the ice cream if our sweet little slave still wants one," he said and brought Anna's luscious lips closer to his, sucking on them gently, and tracing them with his tongue.

"Hmm, " Anna moaned out.

"Do you still want one?" Jackson asked, flipping the vibrator on.

"I.." Anna mumbled, the sizzling pleasure from the vibration was already getting to her, but she summoned courage and nodded. "Yes, I still want one"

Jacob looked at her in amusement and smirked. He likes girls like this, they excite him. "Sure, let's go get the little bunny some ice cream, brother." He uttered, right after spanking Anna's ass.

Getting out of the car was easier than Anna thought, she had thought that she wouldn't be able to stand because Jackson was being a really bad guy. He still kept the vibrator on. Shouldn't he at least turn it off while she's walking?

Anna breathed down heavily as she walked in between the two men inside the ' Amirrino'

"Hello Sir, how can we-

The attendant was about to give out the usual greeting when he spotted the men who just came in with a beautiful lady in a big coat. He was totally bewildered.

Is it winter? Why is she wearing such a big coat? He thought, staring at the lady between them.

"You don't need your eyes anymore?" Jacob interrogated in a deep cold voice, he hated how the man was staring at his slave hungrily. No one can stare at her like that except him and his brother.

"Uhn?" The attendant blinked at the threat and quickly adjusted himself. He looked at the man who threatened him and saw that the man was smiling, but his eyes were cold as the winter. The attendant couldn't help but shiver in fear.

Who the hell was this man? How can someone smile and still look so wicked? He turned his gaze to look at the other man beside him and saw that they were very identical, but unlike the wicked-looking man, the other one looked calm. Maybe not that calm. He reasoned when he saw that the other man too was looking at him as if he wanted to strangle him.

Why are they so strange? He wasn't looking at their woman.

Wait?

Their woman? Did she belong to them both?

Fuck? The attendant's eyes widened in realization.

"Uhm.. hemm. I'm very sorry to say that the store is currently book for the next two hours, you can come back after two hours, we -

"It was booked by us," Jackson interrupted the man in a cold voice. He doesn't have a good impression about the guy. He hated how he was staring visibly at Anna.

"Oh, okay. Please wait, let me confirm." The attendant replied curtly and checked the monitor after Jackson offered his name.

After a few minutes, he looked from the monitor and breathed down slowly glancing at the men in front of him.

They are THE MICHEALSON TWINS!!

He blinked and quickly offered numerous apologies after going through his head again to see if he hadn't misspoken.

The wicked man must be the legendary twin brother, "ahh" he scratched his head after they left for their reserved seat. If he had misspoke earlier, he wouldn't have his head on his neck right now. He quickly thanked his stars for being a little retard.

Anna who had a working vibrator inside her all while was slightly trembling as Jacob drew out a chair for her to sit on.

When Jacob saw that Anna was trembling he looked at his brother with a smirk,. "You still have the vibrator on?"

"Uh-huh," Jackson replied with a smirk, almost identical with his brother's as he sat Anna down right beside them.

After a while, they were served the ice cream and Anna's concentration finally returned to something appealing but not sexual.

She briefly took the ice cream and started eating, but this time the two brothers were also eating theirs, and they weren't just staring at her like the other time in their room.

Since, they don't have much ice cream to eat and they also ordered steaks, Jackson and Jacob later had to watch Anna as she eat hers.

Because of their intensive gazes, Anna almost choke on her ice cream when she looked up and Jacob winked at her. She cleared her throats and shyly looked down at her ice cream.

She didn't know why this settings made it seems like they were on a date where in reality she barely know them except from what they shared online and she's also just met them in reality today.

But why did she felt like this was normal?

Anna looked up again, but this she got some Ice cream on her face and it makes her look funny. When the brothers saw it they almost burst out with laughter. Jacob quickly brought out his phone and took a picture of it because it looks really funny and extremely cute, it made him see her goofy despite her innocent face.

"Why are you taking a picture of me?" Anna asked, blinking her gorgeous eyes. She can't let them take pictures of her!

What if,

Her head couldn't think about the what if's at the moment but she knew that it was very dangerous.

Jacob smirked and slowly moved closer to Anna and gently cleaned the ice cream on her face with his thumb and dipped it inside Anna's mouth, making her suck on his finger as he held her whole face in his hand.

He looked at her face which looked so strangely hot to him at the moment and he suddenly wished that it was his dick that was in her mouth instead of his thumb.

Anna blinked again repeatedly because of the sudden intrusion of her mouth, until she suddenly tasted ice cream on his thumb. She gently licked it off because she tasted the sweetness of the ice cream on it, but she didn't know that her action would bring a groan out of Jacob.

Jacob felt his dick tightened by the lick and his thoughts immediately scattered.

"Jackson, how about we forget the damn steaks and leave." He asked, but his brother only laughed out in excitement.

It was really fun to see his brother impatiently, he always had this sluggish and slow patience for their pets but now he couldn't wait to devour Anna.

"Alright, I will ask for a takeout," Jackson retorted and Anna started wondering why she couldn't eat her ice cream.

Didn't they just get here a few minutes back? Why are leaving so soon?

And they didn't even allow her to finish her ice cream? She stubbornly thought until she remembered that she hadn't felt the pulsation of the vibrator inside her for a while.

Did he turn it off? Anna thought, throwing a gaze at Jackson.

She doesn't even know what's with him and vibrators.

"Are we going back home?" Anna asked, surprising herself that she now thought of their place as home.

She wanted to caution herself but she had already said the words and it cannot be retracted.

"Home...?" Jacob repeated her words and look at his brother but Jackson didn't shared the same thoughts as him because there was an evident frown on his face.

Jacob looked away from his brother and turned to the naive girl between them. "Yeah, we are going home. Don't you wanna remove that stuff inside you," He asked, diverting the conversation.

Immediately Jackson heard his brother's last words, he remembered that there was still a vibrator in Anna's pussy. He looked at the object and saw that he had switched it off.

It must have been when he wanted to eat the ice cream. He thought.

He was aware of the gaze Jacob gave him when Anna said "home" but he wasn't sure if he ready for that yet. And for crying out loud, they just saw the girl today for the first time.

And she's Married, the fact that she was still tied to another man is an urgent issue they had to resolve first.

"What is the name of your husband again?" Jackson asked suddenly, snapping Anna out of her thoughts.

"Danish, " Anna answered, while Jacob opened the car for her to get in.

"Sounds Indianish to me, " Jacob joked, turning on the engine of his latest Mercedes-Benz.

"No, he's American, " Anna defended in a straight face, not getting the joke.

Jackson was immediately irritated when he saw how she was defending her so called husband and a sudden urge to punish her swelled in his head.

"Do you like him that much?" he asked, totally forgotten that Anna said the man hasn't touched her before.

Anna blinked at the sudden question as she looked at the cold face of Jackson.

Like who? Her husband? She was sold to him because her father owed him a huge sum of money!

How did it connect in Jackson's brain that she might possibly like him?

Because of the late reply, Jackson got annoyed and roughly pulled Anna closer to him. "If you like him that much, why did you accept our invites? Why did you let us fuck you?" He bellowed, making Anna scream out in fear.

I will be a good girl, please don't hurt me

"Please don't hit, please don't hurt me," Anna mumbled as she trembled slightly.

The words and actions immediately made Jackson stop his actions and he stared at her strangely. Even Jacob who was driving looked in the mirror to see the trembling Anna.

"Anna," Jackson called out softly, rubbing her silky black hair. Why was she so suddenly scared of him? Why did she think that he wanted to hit her? Was it because he shouted at her?

"Please, I will be a good girl, please don't hurt me," Anna whispered again, this time she was shaking her head violently. She had forgotten that she was with the twins, all she could think of at the moment was that someone wanted to hit her and hurt her.

"Anna, Sweetheart. Calm down, I'm not gonna hurt you. I'm never gonna hurt you, I'm sorry I yelled at you, look I'm really sorry." Jackson asserted, rubbing her back and cuddling her in his embrace.

He didn't mean to shout at her, he was just jealous that she actually belonged to another man not them.

Yes, he was jealous. It took so much of his ego to accept that fact, but he was definitely jealous of that prick of her husband.

After a while, Anna finally calmed down and she slept off in Jackson's arms.

"Brother, did you think her husband used to maltreat and abuse her?" Jackson asked Jacob who was now looking very grim unlike his usual smirking self.

"No, I don't think so. The marks on her body don't look like they were new and she said she just got married to her husband, " Jacob answered, as he remembered the tiny marks he had seen on Anna's body while he was bathing her earlier. The marks were so tiny and non-existent that Anna probably thought they couldn't see them, but he had seen them and he had also counted a bit of it.

Whoever gave her those marks will pay dearly for it.

"So who did you think gave her those marks?" Jackson asked but Jacob just shook his head. He didn't know who it was exactly at the moment, but what he knew was that they would pay dearly for inflicting pain on her.

"Did you think we are rushing things with her," Jackson asked his brother again, after they got down from the car and Jacob offered to carry Anna inside the mansion.

The sky was already pitch dark, as they left quite late before and they spent more than 2 hours outside.

"Whether we are going too far or not, we will get to know in the nearest future but at the moment, I think we need to get her to sleep." Jacob answered and they proceeded inside the master room.

When they got inside, Jacob gently pulled the big black off Anna's body and gently covered her with a big blanket, and left the room with his brother.

"Are you still hungry? I have the take-out with me, " Jackson asserted, showing his brother the steaks he had ordered to be packed.

"Yeah, let's eat, " Jacob replied. At the moment his mind was occupied with Anna's previous actions.

She didn't look like the Anna he knew at all, she was also shy and naughty but that side of her scared the hell out of him.

She looked like she could break down.

"I think you should not shout at her anymore, " Jacob said to his brother suddenly after he concluded.

"Anna, right? I've also thought of that. I didn't know that it would bring that reaction out from her. It was totally unexpected, " Jackson replied, putting some steaks in his mouth and nodding his head at his brother.

"She looked so scared of us, fuck. How much pain had she gone through that could have brought that reaction out of her?" Jacob asked in a cold voice, suddenly losing interest in the food.

"Brother, we can't do anything about the past but we can help her change the future, " Jackson answered but he started thinking about the weight of his words.

How can they help her change the future? He knew that he and his brother weren't ready to have a girlfriend or anything serious at the moment. Even though their parents are nagging at them to find a partner, they just can't bring themselves to be committed to one girl.

Especially Jacob, the status of his job is very risky. As a Mafia boss, a girlfriend means weakness and Anna might be put in danger if his brother's opponents knew that she was their girlfriend.

So helping her or changing the future might be more dangerous to Anna than easy for her.

"Did you think we should just keep her in the house?" Jacob asked suddenly since he saw that his intelligent brother couldn't come up with anything as the solution.

Totally defeated and unable to think of a better idea, Jackson replied. "I think that's better for now,"

"But wouldn't she have to go back to her husband?" Jacob asked after a while when he remembered that she was still married and it wasn't to them.

"Well..can we not think about that for now? Who knows if her so-called husband would even come back after five months," Jackson replied.

He hates thinking about the fact that Anna was still married. It always gets on his nerves. He didn't even want to ever remember it.

"Alright, I have to travel tomorrow. I have to go and inspect the guns coming in from Italy. Christian can't do it alone and I know that his new wife is a big distraction to him." Jacob announced after a while. Christian was his second in command and he was the one that always oversees the mafia anytime Jacob wasn't around.

"What about the others? No one can oversee it while you aren't around?" Jackson asked. Honestly, he didn't really know anyone other than Christian since he wasn't interested in the Mafia world, but he was also skillfully trained in combat by their father, he had channeled his own as self-protection.

"No they can't, " Jacob answered.

Jackson nodded and heaved a deep sigh, he knew that his brother's work was far more stressful and dangerous than his, but he also knew that he can't make decisions for him.

Jacob had chosen the rough and Mafia life since they were eighteen, he had fought through thick and thin with blood in his hands before he could attain the position he was at the moment and he deserved every bit of power and position he was at the moment.

"When are you leaving tomorrow?" Jackson asked.

"Not early though, I still have to take our little slave out while you go to work. I will leave when you get back so I can hang her over to you, " Jacob replied with a half-smirk. His usual playfulness was now evident.

"Where did you intend to take her?" Jackson asked, but Jacob only smirked.

"Don't tell me you are leaving me out of the fun?" Jackson asserted but his brother only chuckled.

"Calm down, I'm not taking her that far. Just the vacation house at Manchester. You know I can't take her to the public without endangering her life. I don't want her to be targeted," Jacob answered slowly, replying to his eager brother. "Don't worry. We will send you some pictures," He added, making Jackson scowl.

"Don't send me pictures," Jackson refused outrightly. He knew what his brother wanted to do.

He probably wanted to rub it in his face tomorrow but he wouldn't give in.

Jackson suddenly thought of not going to work tomorrow but quickly discarded the idea. If he didn't go to work, Linda would probably think that he had died or something because it would be his first time ever.

"Are you sure you really don't want any pictures?" Jacob taunted his brother with a smirk but Jackson ignored him and took the empty takeout to the bin.

"Don't you think you should worry more about the smuggling of your guns? Instead of taunting me with pictures?" Jackson answered, frowning at his brother but Jacob only shrugged.

"There's nothing to worry about. I already secured the deal before I left, I'm only going there to oversee it and I'm sure they wouldn't want to play any foul play because who would want to do that with my goods? Are they tired of living?" Jacob asserted, and Jackson nodded.

If he envied anything about his twin brother, it would be his aura and confidence which he knew he must have gained from years of experience and bloodshed.

Even though his brother might look like a devil or in fact a nemesis to other people, he was still his twin brother, his duplicate, and his closest family and he would always support him.

"What are you doing? Looking at me all glossy? Let's go to bed, " Jacob said to Jackson who was lost in thought. "Did you think our little slave will be lonely in bed?" he suddenly asked, looking at his brother.

"Let's go and check, " Jackson answered, partnering his thoughts as he led the way to the master's room again.

When they got inside, they couldn't believe their sight.

Eating Anna out; Breaching the contract

Anna was asleep, but her nightgown strap had already fallen off. Making her enormous breasts leak out of the nightgown, it was peeping out of the nightgown as if they had escaped an entrapment.

The duvet that Jacob had covered her body with was already abandoned and she was just laying there on the bed with her left breast out and her right nipples transparent to their naked eyes.

"This girl will be the death of me," Jackson let out slowly when he saw the reaction his body was responding to the erotic girl in front of him.

"And me too, " Jacob seconded.

Since Jackson was closer to the bed, he was able to get to Anna faster than his brother. But Jacob wasn't rushing, he was slowly discarding his clothes unlike his impatient brother who was running to get the breast in his mouth.

Anna moaned softly when she felt a large hand slowly fondlingbher breast, she was still sound asleep but her body was already reacting to the sizzling sexual attention she was receiving.

"Hmmm, " She muttered and arched closer to the hand that was touching her.

"Are you sure she's still asleep, " Jackson asked his brother who was now naked and was already on the bed with them.

"There's only one way to find out, " Jacob answered, then he slowly parted Anna's soft thighs and inserted a finger inside her pussy.

"Hmmm...I think she's really asleep, but she's damn wet, " he answered after bringing out his finger and seeing how drenched it was.

What excites him most about their new sex slave was that, she was always wet and ready for them. Anytime.

He likes how responsive and wet she always was for them. And it always drives him crazy.

"Do you think we should wake her up?" Jackson asked, softly squeezing Anna's breast. At the moment, he can't wait for her to wake up and look at him with her soulful eyes as he inserted his cock inside her mouth.

There was something about how she looked at him that always undoes him and he couldn't wait to experience that again and again.

"No, let her wake up and be surprised, " Jacob answered, nudging his dick inside Anna's entrance and coating it with her dripping juice. It was so silky that he almost rammed his way inside her wet pussy.

Slowly, he delved inside her and groaned roughly when Anna moaned out in her sleep.

"She's not awake yet, " Jackson told his brother, but Jacob couldn't hear him anymore. This was the first time he was inside Anna's pussy and he felt that he never wished to come out.

He totally wanted to own her and make her submit to his will. Unable to take it anymore, he raised his hands to her neck and choked her while slamming his dick inside her.

"Ahhh, " Anna jolted awake immediately from the sudden intrusion, but Jacob didn't wait for her to get used to his dick before he continued thrusting deep and faster while choking her.

"Ahh, yess, " Anna moaned out incoherently, she was having a happy dream about having sex and roleplaying with the twin and the dream was so sweet that she didn't want to wake up. But she actually woke up to this, she couldn't be more grateful.

She already forgot about what had happened before she had fall asleep on Jackson shoulders, she looked up and saw that Jackson was looking at her being choked and fucked by his brother with a small smile tugging at his lips.

Did he enjoy it that much? Looking at her while his twin brother fuck her?

Should she play with him a bit and see if he can still maintain that smile? Anna thought to herself.

But would he punish her and yell at her again? She doesn't want to-

"Ahhhhhh, " she moaned out in pleasure, her thought was interrupted by Jacob's constant thrusts and she couldn't even think straight anymore.

She loved how he was holding her neck and choking her while he fucked her from behind. It was so pleasurable that she wanted to shout more and she did exactly as she wanted.

"More...!" She let out and Jackson chuckled throatily.

"Brother, the little slut said she wants more." He told his brother, and Jacob instantly flipped Anna on her knees, making her face Jackson while he fucked her from behind. He still had his hand around her neck, choking her.

At the moment, Anna definitely regretted shouting more, because she was now given more than she could handle. She could feel that Jacob was now touring her womb and he was bringing her to ultimate pleasure.

"I'm- ahhh, " She stuttered and groaned out in pleasure.

Jackson came closer to her and slapped her chubby cheeks softly, "You are what? Talk little fucking whore,"

"I'm gonna cum... I'm gonna cum, " Anna managed to let out, but her upper body was instantly raised up by Jacob and he whispered in her left ear.

"If you cum without my permission, I will have Jackson insert the vibrator in your pussy till the next morning," He threatened and let her body fall on the bed again.

It excites her, the way they talk to her and make her feel like a slut, she loves it. She really loves it.

At the moment, she couldn't even be bothered by how naughty and devious their words were or how they were using her body.

She couldn't even bring herself to think that she was married and she didn't belong to them.

What she wanted right now was used by the twin brothers.

"I want your dick in my mouth," She said to Jackson, who looked at her with a smirk on his face.

"Did you hear that? Our little slut finally requested something from us, " Jackson told his brother. "How bad did you want it? Maybe if you show me and tell me how bad you want it, I might fulfil your wishes, " He added cockily and Anna almost groaned out from the sexy way he said those words.

"I really want you to put your dick in my mouth, " Anna managed to breathe out of her mouth because Jacob's hands were still on her neck.

Jacob slowly pulled out his hardened dick when he saw that Anna was struggling to say the word she wanted to say and let her fall on the bed.

He stood up from the bed and went to where his brother was. Anna immediately felt the absence of his huge dick in her pussy and she almost cried out.

But she could see it now, it was dripping off her juice.

"What are you looking at? Ain't you gonna suck it?" Jacob asked and his brother laughed out loud.

"Gently brother, she had to be taught. You know she was a virgin just yesterday, she probably don't know that she had to suck off her own cum, "

"Now that I tell you little slut, I guess you know what to do right?" Jacob asked and Anna quickly scrambled off the bed, with her eyes opened.

She raised her gorgeous eyes at Jacob and gradually cupped his member in her hands and took it in her mouth.

Jacob groaned throatily in pleasure when he felt her soft tongue on his cap. He honestly didn't know what he enjoyed most. If it was her pussy or her wet mouth.

While they were at it, Jackson went on the bed and gently spread Anna's thigh again. Anna who was instantly happy that she was about to be fucked again was surprised when she felt Jackson's hand on her hips and gently drawing her down on him.

Because she had Jacob 's dick on her mouth, she couldn't turn around to see what Jackson was doing with her waist until she felt something flickering her fold.

Wait? What's that? She trembled in pleasure from the sizzling electricity.

Jacob, who was enjoying Anna's mouth and tongue, was immediately discarded by Anna because she couldn't bring herself to concentrate anymore. The flickers were getting more frequent and her entire body was shaming with uncontrollable desire.

"Get back to what you are doing, " Jacob groaned, when he saw that she was distracted.

"I can't, " Anna answered shakily, she was shivering from head to toe. She loves his big dick in her mouth but she just couldn't focus because of what Jackson was doing with her pussy.

Is he eating her out? Wasn't it stated in the contract that they wouldn't eat her pussy?

Then why was he breaching the contract now?

When Jacob saw that desire was building in her eyes and she really couldn't stand it anymore, he held her hair and brought her head closer to his dick. Dipping his dick in her mouth while she moaned out from pleasure.

"Ouuuu ahhh," Anna mumbled as tears flew out from her gorgeous eyes. She was being choked by the younger twin while the eldest was eating her out.

The pleasure was so exhilarating that she couldn't help but succumb to the pleasure and let the wave drive her to the peak.

"Shit, I got her juices all over my face," Jackson let out.

A/N: Jackson is breaching the contract. *scoffs* horny little fowl.

Yes, I'm such a good slut

"Shit, I got her juices all over my face," Jackson let out.

After managing to spit out those words, Jackson used his fingers to wipe Anna's cum on his face and licked his hands off.

Anna, who was completely exhausted, was about to fall on Jackson's face when Jacob bit his lip and groaned as shot his cum deep inside her mouth.

"Ahh, fuck, " Jacob groaned and Anna suck off his dick, "You are such a good little slut, aren't you?" He muttered, his voice so deep that Anna's body shivered in reaction.

"You should answer when he talks to you, " Jackson interjected, shifting off and letting Anna rest on the bed.

"Yes, I am," Anna replied after hearing Jackson's words, but Jacob furrowed his brows in a deep frown.

"That's not how to answer a question, reply as you mean it, " he held Anna's face and saw that she still had a little bit of his cum under her bottom lip.

"Yes, I'm such a good slut, " Anna answered. She slowly looked at Jacob and licked her mouth shyly.

Coincidentally, her tongue reached where the cum was, and she licked it off too. Making Jacob groan out. At the moment, he didn't want anything more than to slap her cheeks and make her feel like a good slut and his dick tightened again in an erection.

This slutty little whore will be the death of him, everything she does drives him crazy.

"You need a bath, " Jacob said slowly, rubbing Anna's cheeks while applying pressure on it. The action was slightly turning her on but she couldn't say anything since they just had a very intense sex.

If they knew that she's horny again, would that make her seem like a whore? Well, not that there's something wrong in being their whore but she will just have to keep it in for now.

"She's not the only one that needs a bath, we all we'd to shower," Jackson replied and his brother nodded.

Picking up Anna in his arms, Jacob carried her into the large bathroom. It was huge and big, Anna could see how spacious it was.

At first she had thought that they would allow her to take her bath herself and she would be able to extinguish the fire blazing in her body but it seems that the twins can't keep their hands off her body.

They entrapped her between them again and Jacob started rubbing soap on her body while his brother was slowly palming her breast. He was probably helping her scrub and he might not mean the action to be sexual, but she was feeling so hot and excited deep in her core.

If they touch her now, they would be surprised at how wet she was and it's definitely not from the shower.

Unable to keep the tension to herself anymore, Anna breathed out. "Hmm, ahh, "

"What is it, little slut. Are we making you horny again?" Jacob who was just applying soap on her body was instantly intrigued by her soft moan.

"No, I just feel a bit trapped, " Anna muttered, looking away and letting the shower pour on her head. Immediately cleaning all the foamy soap on her body. Now Jackson had nothing to play with except her bare breasts, which she immediately regretted.

She had thought that if there wasn't any soap on her body, the twins would focus on the bath and she wouldn't be so hot and tingling anymore, but it looks like she was the only one that thinks that way.

"Your breasts, they are so big and succulent. I wanna taste them every now and then, " Jackson muttered, calming Anna's breasts in his hands and giving it a rough squeeze. Making Anna groan in pleasure.

"I thought you said we aren't making you horny, " Jacob asked, chuckling and smashing Anna's round ass.

"I uhmm- I" Anna mumbled, unable to come up with a reply. She was beyond good reasoning, if she says a word now, it might be a plea for them to fuck her.

"How did you get these scars, " Jacob asked, touching her ribs and Anna flinched. The question immediately removed any sexual thinking in her mind

How did they see the scars? She thought it had disappeared. She had even bought some cleaning cream from her husband's credit card because she doesn't want to be seen with those scars anymore.

"Scars?" She asked, feigning ignorance which made Jacob mad. He hates when people pretend or take his questions slightly.

Anna might not know but this is one of the first five laws on his Mafia gang.

Never pretend, say it as it is. If not, the member would be killed immediately.

"Those scars on your body, or do you think we wouldn't notice? Though it's very tiny, it's still a bit obvious, " Jackson answered, and Anna sniffed.

She's not ready to tell them anything about her life. She just came here to be sexually used. Maybe physically too if it brings her pleasure and nothing more.

She is not here to have a heart-to-heart talk with them.

"It's nothing, they are just childhood scars, " Anna replied after a few minutes and Jacob frowned.

What the fuck! Those scars don't look a fucking childhood scars. He almost shouted at her before he remembered what had happened when Jackson had shouted at her earlier so he kept his words to himself.

If he finds out that it was her husband that inflicted those wounds on her and she's protecting him. He won't be able to keep his useless life.

The conversation made everything awkward and the bath became brief as the twins focused on the bath after a few minutes. Even though that's what Anna wanted, she wasn't expecting it to be so abrupt.

After a few minutes, Jackson wrapped her body in a towel while Jacob brought another nightgown for her to wear. Looking at the clock on the wall, Anna could see that it was almost 2 am. It's already so late.

Tomorrow, she must leave here and be on her way to her husband's house. Everything is already getting too overwhelming and intrusive. Now the Twins wanted to know more about her life when what they had agreed on was just sexual pleasures.

She married and she can't leave her husband because she was sold to him by her father. And he mustn't even get wind about what she's doing right now else, she couldn't even imagine what would happen.

She had given her virginity to the twin, and they had fucked her repeatedly. Her pussy definitely wouldn't be the same as someone who was just disvirgined anymore. She just hoped that her husband didn't arrive tomorrow or any day sooner so her hole can close up a bit before he comes back so she can lie and tell him that she had used a dildo on herself.

"What are you thinking about so intensely?" Jackson asked, he was the observant twin.

"Nothing, " Anna muttered in a low voice, making Jacob turn his gaze at her.

"If she doesn't want to talk, leave her alone" He replied, he was still obviously annoyed about what happened in the bathroom but Anna didn't mind.

No matter how angry or annoyed he is, she wouldn't tell them anything about her personal life not because she feels ashamed of it but because she doesn't want their pity.

"I'm going to bed, " Anna mumbled, and Jackson tucked her in and slept beside her. Cuddling her body to his. He had looked at the time earlier and saw that it was already late. He had to wake up early tomorrow morning, so he should sleep now.

Jacob, who was still very much angry, couldn't bring himself to sleep at the moment. His head just couldn't stop thinking about the traces of marks on Anna's body and how she had been defiant about it.

He went back into the sitting room and opened one of the drawers to bring some weed out of the bag and crushed them with his crusher, then rolled two sticks up. He needs the smoke right now. Without it , he might not be able to stay sane.

Lighting up his weeds, he started puffing them when he heard Anna's phone beeped up.

He went closer to where it was, expecting to see another message or call from her so called husband but it was her social media notifications and someone just sent her a message saying "Nice boobs, you got there,"

Jacob instantly flinched and screenshotted the profile then sent it to Christian.

"Teach him a very good lesson," He captioned and Christian immediately replied. "Yes, Boss,"

Since it was late and almost 3 am, someone would have thought that Christian would be asleep by now but he wasn't and Jacob was grateful for that. At least now he can be at rest that he was taking good care of the Mafia family in his absence.

"Boss, are you still coming tomorrow?" Christian asked, texting Jacob.

Puffing and dragging his weed, Jacob opened the message and thought for a while.

He had planned on taking Anna to the vacation house tomorrow but he's currently angry at her, he doesn't know whether to still take her or not.

Do you want to be choked by something else?

Got the image above from Pinterest, if you are not freaky enough, skip the next chapter ****When Anna woke the next morning, she didn't see any of the twins and was slightly happy about the news. They shouldn't be around, she will just take her bath and leave quietly.

When she gets back to her husband's house safely, she will delete her profile and then app, and she will forget everything about the twins.

It's for the best.

Anna convinced herself as she dragged herself up from the bed and looked at herself in the nearest mirror. She realized that she was still wearing the second nightgown Jacob had worn for her before he got mad at her.

She quickly removed the nightgown and went inside the bathroom she had shared with the twins the previous night to take her bath, but in the process she couldn't stop herself from thinking about what had happened in the bathroom.

Did she make a mistake? But how did they even see the scars? She had used a cleaning oil to make them less visible.

Anna looked inside the bathroom mirror to check the scars again but she can't even see them herself.

What was she even worrying about? if she leaves now, she wouldn't ever see them again. So why is she so concerned about how they knew about her scars? They didn't even know her outside social media, they can't even trace her.

So it's very easy for her to disappear, she just has to delete the stupid Tumblr app. She convinced herself again.

After taking her bath, Anna searched for her clothes but found out that it wasn't in the master room. That was when she remembered that they didn't make it to the master's room at first yesterday.

They had stripped her in the sitting room and fucked her right there after she had signed the consent form. It was later that they brought her into the master's room.

Telling herself not to remember how she was used and fucked by the twins, Anna zeroed her mind and went out of the master room.

Her big brown eyes widened when she saw Jacob smoking in the sitting room, looking delicious with the blunt in his mouth. Totally forgetting the intention of coming outside to get her clothes and her escape plan, Anna couldn't draw her eyes away from Jacobs's physical frame, and how sexy he looked while he was smoking.

"Are you looking at me or the blunt?" Jacob asked, after noticing Anna's presence in the sitting room and also how she was staring at him. He looked at her and saw she looked refreshed and she was only putting on a towel.

She looked so savory and sexy in the towel, and it was barely covering much since her inner thighs were still fully visible to his naked eyes.

"Come here, " Jacob beaconed to Anna slowly after taking a drag from his weed and puffing it out.

Anna looked at him and wished that he had puffed it on her face instead, she missed the feeling of getting high. The last night she smoked was the day she left her father 's house after he slapped and kicked her around.

She moved closer to Jacob and sat beside him on the sofa, but he shook his head and patted his lap, indicating that he wanted her to sit on his lap which she reluctantly agreed to. Now sitting on his laps with one of his hands wrapped around her waist, Anna didn't know she was feeling hot because of the smoke that he's now puffing on her face or because of his hand that was slowly rubbing her waist.

"Do you smoke?" Jacob asked.

"Yeah, not usually though, " Anna replied, when she smokes, it's usually from her father's pack of cigarettes and she always makes sure that he doesn't know about it. So it was always one stick in three weeks.

"You want a drag?" He asked, passing the blunt to her and she slowly accepted it and took a slow drag from it but she ended up roughly badly.

"Slow down, little slut. This isn't the usual strain." Jacob said, and quickly patted her back and also chuckled at how cute she looked. Her face was all red, but he still found it appealing and sexy. "You try though, that was a nice drag, " He complimented and Anna's cheeks flushed in embarrassment.

"How are you feeling now? Are you okay?" He asked, and Anna struggled to answer, but the smoke was still in her throat.

"Wait, here. Let me get you some water, " Jacob mumbled and gently placed Anna on the sofa and went to the fridge to get her water and also a drink for himself.

"Here, have it, " He offered Anna a glass and she quickly took a gulp, but because of her she rushed it. Some of it fell on the towel and it became wet.

Jacob's attention slowly moved from her mouth, then to her wet towel and he couldn't help but get hard just by thinking about removing that towel.

"Are you okay now?" He asked again, also taking a full from his drink to soothe his already blazing desire.

He lightened up his weed again and dragged it out but this time, he didn't ask Anna to take a drag anymore and she couldn't help but feel sad. She had actually enjoyed the blunt.

"Where's Jackson?" Anna asked, after noticing that it was only Jacob that was around.

"Haha, I thought you would never ask, " Jacob chuckled softly.

It was when Anna heard his reply, that she remembered what she came out for. She came outside to pick up her clothes and leave the mansion.

"Where are my clothes?" She asked Jacob, and a frown appeared on his face. He enjoyed looking at her like this and he couldn't even get enough, but she still wanted to put on clothes?

"What for?"

"To wear, of course." Anna replied, but she didn't tell him that she was going home because she didn't know how he would react.

"Yeah, I know that. What I'm asking is why do you have to wear clothes? If you feel uncomfortable in the towel, you can remove it, " Jacob countered, leaving Anna with no choice than to shut her mouth up.

With the way he was looking at her, she knew that if she removed the towel, his attention wouldn't be on the weed in his hand again. She will be the one that he would be dragging.

No matter how much she wanted him to touch her and have his ways with her, she can't. She had to leave.

She didn't even know if her husband was back home yet, she hadn't touched her phone since the other time he called and she hadn't seen the phone around.

"Do you see my phone around?" She asked Jacob and he brought her phone out of his pocket. Oh, so it was with him all this while?

"What did you want to use the phone for? To call your husband? Or to chat with your Tumblr possible future sex partners?" Jacob asked, unable to keep the jealousy out of his words. Since yesterday when he had seen that dickhead message to her, he hadn't been able to stop smoking and was greatly annoyed.

The fact that they had also met her on the same app, and now they have as their little sex slave was making him feel like those profiles that had pending requests on her profile also had a chance to fuck her, and it was driving him crazy.

Upon hearing his hurtful words, Anna flinched as her heart felt hurt. How could he say that to her?

Just because she came here to see them doesn't mean that she would go and meet other people. She wasn't even planning on coming here to see them if not for their persistence urge and also because she wanted to see and just see what they look like in reality. She was married and she shouldn't be here anyway.

Well, don't you know you were married when they had their dicks in your pussy and mouth? A tiny voice reminded her and she felt her eyes pickled with tears. She just had to leave, she can't stay here anymore.

"Where are my clothes," Anna demanded again, this time she raised her voice a little, and Jacob frowned again.

"Thrown away. If you need a cloth so bad, I can get you a few more, " He answered and Anna frowned.

Thrown away? Why the hell did he throw her clothes away! How will she go home then?

"Why did you throw my clothes away? There wasn't anything wrong with the clothes, I just got them." She retorted, and the towel almost fell off her chest.

"Because they look prudish, I will get you another one. As much as you want."

"I don't want you to get me another one, I don't want you or your brother to buy me things. Why would you throw my clothes away?" Anna asked again, this time, she forced herself to say so much because she was very angry. She didn't even believe that her voice could be as loud as it was. She had never raised her voice at someone since forever, she had even forgotten how it was to be angry at someone. All she had experienced for the last two years was pain and discomfort. Since she couldn't do anything about it she had to obey and be docile.

Deep down, she knew she wasn't really angry at Jacob, but she just felt like her escape plan had been ruined.

"If you shout at me again, you will be punished, " Jacob said to Anna coldly. She could see that she had managed to infuriate him, so she just stared at him blankly. Forcing herself to shut up.

"What? You don't want to be punished? Well, you sure do like it whenever I said I wanted to punish you last night, didn't you?" Jacob asked, raising a brow at Anna and she suddenly felt hot.

No, she mustn't react to this, she must not allow herself to feel hot and excited again. She had to stay angry and leave this mansion.

She had to go back to her husband's house.

When Jacob saw that she wasn't saying anything and was just ignoring him, he dragged his weed and puffed it on her face. Making Anna choke because of how unexpected it was.

"Do you want to be choked by something else?" Jacob asked, pulling the towel off Anna's chest while she choked on the smoke.

Surprise vacation for Anna

"Do you want to be choked by something else?" Jacob asked, pulling the towel off Anna's chest while she choked on the smoke.

Anna blinked as she coughed but when she stopped coughing, Jacob's hands were already on her breasts, folding and squeezing them.

"I need to go back home, " Anna muttered, trying to resist the sexual urge she was feeling from Jacob's hands.

"Home? Uh?" Jacob scoffed, he was angry. Why can't she just forget about home or her useless husband when she's here with them?

"You are here to cheat on your husband, why are you rushing? Aren't we satisfying you enough?" Jacob asked and Anna felt her body reaction rhyming with his brazen words.

Why does she still feel attracted to him so much when all he does was to make her feel like a slut.

No, she can't..she shouldn't like it! She mustn't!

"Jacob please, I need to go home, " Anna muttered, calling him by his name to show how serious she was.

"On your knees, go on your knees. " Jacob ordered in anger, at the moment he couldn't wait to inflict pain on her sexually until she screamed and wanted more like the slut she was.

Immediately Anna heard him order her to go on her knees, she felt her pussy clenched in pleasure and she tried to stop herself from moaning.

She was about to kneel when a phone started ringing. She looked at her phone that was beside her and saw that it was not her phone, so she guessed it was Jacob's.

Fishing his phone out from his pocket, Jacob looked at her and he saw that she was already excited because her eyes looked so seductive at the moment.

"Spread your thighs, " He muttered, and clicked on his phone. Connecting to the call.

Anna glanced at Jacob and gradually did as he wanted, spreading her legs while he feasted his eyes with it when he was on call.

"Okay, sure. Meet me at the vacation house before 7 pm, " Jacob ended the call with Christian who had called to know if he's still coming to the vacation house and if he should still prepare what he had asked him to prepare last night.

"Do you know how juicy your pussy looks right now?" Jacob asked, raising his eyes slightly from Anna's exposed pussy and moved closer to her.

"Why are you so obedient? Do you know how the fuck that turns me on?" He asked Anna, raising her chin up and she blinked.

Anna doesn't know, she just doesn't want to be hit. And she also likes it when he looks at her like that, as if he can't wait to eat her up.

"No," Anna mumbled and before she could close her mouth, Jacob dipped his fingers inside her mouth and she closed her mouth around his fingers, sucking on it.

"Bitch!" Jacob groaned when he felt her saliva on his finger. He thought about bending her over, and fuck her until her voice cracked from screaming, but he shook his head.

No, he can't fuck her right now.

He should restrain himself until they get to the vacation house and she would see what he had prepared for her. He can't wait to see her brown eyes widened in pleasure when she sees it.

Removing his fingers from her mouth, he gently wrapped her nipples between them and squeezed them gently. Anna hissed from pleasure caused by the uncontrollable sexual desires.

Jacob moved his fingers away when he saw that her breathing wasn't in sync anymore.

"You look like this even without me fucking you, and you still think your husband can pleasure you? Hilarious," He chuckled as he commented, making Anna suddenly feel embarrassed.

"How old is your husband?" Jacob asked, sitting opposite Anna and picked up his lighter to light up his abandoned weed.

"And keep your legs open as you answer my questions," he interjected when he saw that Anna was about to close her legs. He didn't want her to. She must open her legs and feel like a slut that she was.

"But, I'm naked, " Anna countered with a pout. He was looking at her exposed body and he was just smoking as if she was a painting while he asked her how old her husband was.

Why is he doing that? Is he trying to make her feel ashamed or what?

"I know that you are. I want you to be naked, that was why I removed the towel you were putting on, " Jacob answered with a shrug, he looked unbothered.

Swallowing up her other words, Anna cleared her throat and answered. "I don't know how old he is. We just got married." She answered, she didn't even know why she had added that piece of information about 'just got married.'

It wasn't as if she was in an interview.

"Oh, just got married? So he should be the one that inflicted those scars on you right?" Jacob countered, remembering the scars and yesterday's incident.

Definitely, he wasn't the only one who remembered what happened yesterday. Even Anna instantly remembered and felt sad and embarrassed. She doesn't like talking about it at all.

When Jacob saw her change of mood, he looked at her and frowned.

"Who is that person you are protecting so badly? Is he your past lover?" He asked, frustrated by her silence. He hated that she kept on protecting someone who had given her so many scars. Most of them look more than ordinary marks.

Couldn't she see that he was trying to protect her?

But how can Jacob know that it wasn't a past lover, but her biological father and it wasn't that she didn't want to talk about it but she dared not?

Picking up his phone disheartened, he dialed Christain's phone and asked him to order some female clothes and waybill it to the mansion.

"Okay boss," Christian replied and waited patiently for his boss to hang up. But all this while he was wondering who was the new lady that caught his boss's attention.

It wasn't up to an hour when the clothes were delivered and Jacob asked Anna to dress up in the outfit.

When Anna saw the outfit, she was beyond surprised because it technically looked like a practical 'submissive' costume she had seen on the internet and it barely covered anything.

Why is Jacob asking her to wear this? Does he want her to walk around in the house with this?

When Anna came out dressed in the costume, Jacob almost lost his senses.

"This...." he became tongue-tied and Anna blinked at him not understanding why he was looking at her that way.

Wasn't he the one that asked her to wear the cloth? So why is he acting surprised?

But how would she know that Jacob had just asked Christian to get a good outfit and this was all his idea.

"Do I look weird in it?" Anna asked when she saw that Jacob was still looking at her.

"Weird? Why the hell would you look weird? The only thing that's not completing this outfit is a choker on your neck, " He muttered, and Anna gave him a quizzical look, not understanding what he was saying.

"Don't worry, you will understand when we get to where we are going?" Jacob asserted when he saw her confused look.

"We are going somewhere?" Anna asked, blinking in shock. She thought he wanted her to wear this inside the house!

She can't go out like this!

Her body is barely covered apart from the long leather boot that was up to her knees, her remaining outfits are barely covering her body. Especially her breasts, it was almost spilling out and the skirt was way too short.

"Yeah? What?" Jacob asked, raising his eyebrows at her.

That was when Anna noticed that Jacob was also dressed. He was now putting on a shirt and pants but the first two buttons were not hooked.

"I can't go out like this, " Anna whispered and knotted her hands together. She hasn't dressed in an outfit like this before in her entire life. Now he wants her to go out like that?

"Don't worry, there's no one apart from us in this whole mansion and you will be in the car throughout the journey." Jacob replied, looking at her shy face and instantly felt like pinching her red cheeks.

Why does she look so adorable?

"Are we going to meet Jackson?" Anna asked, since that was the only thing she could think of, she hadn't seen Jackson since she had woken up and Jacob hadn't said where they were going so she had assumed they wanted to go and see his twin brother. Her other daddy.

"You missed him, uh?" Jacob asked, giving his usual evil smirk.

"Yes, " Anna replied, unable to stop herself from replying. They balanced each other. She doesn't know what it is but she feels incomplete when the twins aren't inside her or with her.

Suddenly she felt like she might never be able to forget about them even if she left the mansion and went back to her husband's house.

No, she has to forget about them! No matter what, she had to forget about them and concentrate on her marital life.

"Besides, the pill you gave me yesterday, what is meant for?"

Hey guys, I have intentions of creating a bookTube account, where you can listen to short clips of my book audio. Check my wall on my profile for the link, and let me know in the comment section.

TT can't stop me.

What's a choker?

"What pill? Oh- that, so you won't get knocked up." Jacob replied, arching a brow at Anna, "don't tell me you thought it was an aphrodisiac drug? Haha" He laughed and Anna's face flushed red as she quickly looked away.

He was right, she had actually thought for a brief second that all her previous actions were induced by a drug because whenever she remembered how submissive, and horny she was feeling those times, she couldn't bring herself to think she was the one.

"Come on little whore, it was ALL you back then." Jacob laughed again, flashing his wicked smirk.

"Aren't we leaving anymore?" Anna asked when she saw that Jacob was looking at her as if she was a whole diet.

Jacob raised his hand and gently touched Anna's reddened cheek, he was amused by her innocence. "Let's go." He answered and gently took Anna's hands and they both left the gigantic living room. When they got to the garage, Anna's eyes almost popped out from surprise when she saw different kinds of expensive cars. It was as if they went to a car dealer garage, instead of a house garage.

"All these cars belong to you?" Anna asked, her voice filled with wonder. She has never seen so many cars altogether.

"No, just this beauty. I like guns more. They all belong to Jackson. He has a limousine too." Jacob replied when he saw that the Limo wasn't present in the garage. "He probably went to work with it," He added.

"He went to work?" Anna asked, facing Jacob, and he chuckled, opening the passenger's seat for Anna. "Of course, why else do you think he will leave your wet ass pussy?" He countered.

Anna blushed at his naughty words and decided to just ignore him, "What about you? You don't work?" she asked as Jacob turned on the engine.

"I do." Jacob answered, he replied driving out of the mansion.

"Then why didn't you go to work?"

When she woke up and didn't see the twins, she had thought that they'd gone to work or something. So, she had started planning her escape until she came out and saw Jacob taking a blunt.

"You can't resist my wet ass pussy?" Anna asked after testing the words in her mouth to sound as Jacob had sounded earlier.

"Ouu, where did that come from? I like this." A mischievous glint flashed in Jacob's dark eyes as he replied. He took a glance at Anna's shy face, "we have different jobs. I can't work in an office."

"So your job is not in the office?" Anna mumbled, nodding in her head. She had noticed that his personality doesn't fit a CEO unlike Jackson's.

"No, can you guess my work?" Jacob asked and Anna shook her head.

"I'm not good at making a guess, I'd probably say you are a police man." Anna replied and quickly looked away. She just noted that she had been having a proper conversation with Jacob and she was free with him which was unlike herself.

"Police man? how did you come to that?" Jacob grunted, furrowing his brows. What the hell, he was a lawbreaker. How could he still be a policeman? That was a No for him.

"Because...Because.." Anna found out that she saw she couldn't bring herself to say the words. She was actually thinking because they like to discipline her, maybe one of them was a policeman. She couldn't possibly say this to him right? What would he think she was?

"What is it little slut, don't wanna tell me," Jacob countered, pulling along to the driveway of the vacation house.

"Where is this place?" Anna asked, finally concentrating on every-thing else apart from the thoughts in her head, the house they were in currently looked so unique and different. Totally different from the mansion they were coming from which looked glamorous.

"This is uhmm.. Never mind, I call it the vacation house. It usually takes about four months before I bring anyone here. But I don't know why I decided to bring you today. Jackson would have loved to come too but he can't, so I promised that we will be doing a premium live video for him." Jacob replied, as if Jackson had actually begged for it.

"Alright, " Anna replied, not knowing that Jacob wanted to use the video to taunt his brother.

"Let's go in. Jacob said to Anna before getting down to open the front seat for her.

When they got inside, the interior designers were even more odd and different from the outside. "You had them do this too?" Anna asked, pointing at the wallpapers that looked different and unique.

"Yes, do you like it?" Jacob asked, pausing beside Anna to see the wallpaper he had actually put on himself because he didn't want anyone to appreciate the view before him.

"It's different, " Anna mumbled, saying the first thing that came to her mouth.

"Yeah, that's what I wanted. What do you wanna eat? Steaks? Take out? Chinese?" Jacob asked, "or Ice cream" he added when he remembered the previous night.

"No. Just pizza, " Anna replied, she didn't know why she suddenly had the urge to eat pizza.

"Alright, cool, " Jacob adhered, thinking about how good she would look eating pizza in her current outfit. He really needs to find a choker for that outfit.

"Hello Christian, get few boxes of pizzas when you are coming, and find me a fucking choker. " Jacob said when his phone connected after dialing his subordinate's number.

"Okay boss, " he replied.

"What's a choker," Anna asked innocently.

"Curious? You will see when he brings it, " Jacob replied with a deliberate smirk, and left to get himself a wine.

Most of the time, he was always out of London but whenever he felt like coming home. This place always comes to his mind, and that's if Jackson was out of town. Maybe it was because he did most of the designs himself.

"I'm not curious, " Anna replied when Jacob got back with a glass of champagne, but her flushed ears were visible to him.

"Come closer, " he called out as if summoning a pet.

"No, wait. Get on your knees and come closer." Jacob growled when something got his attention.

"Uhn?" Anna blinked her eyes at him. He wants her to crawl to him? Is he joking?

"Get on your knees and come?" Jacob ordered again, but now in a more dominant voice and Anna instantly felt wet.

A/NSkip the next two chapters if you are not a fan of degradation, Alcohol, and rough sexual intercourse.

Pre-show for Anna

SPOILER!!An excerpt from chapter 55

"Get on your knees and come?" Jacob said again, but now in a more dominant voice and Anna instantly felt wet.

Getting on her knees, Anna looked at Jacob and slowly crawled towards him until her face was brushing his bulge and he groaned.

"You are making it hard to wait for Christian to come before I fuck you," Jacob muttered, grabbing her chin and Anna blinked at him.

"Who's Christian?" She asked, is it another brother? God, is he going to fuck her too? Will this turn her into a slut? Anna thought and quickly shook her head.

She doubts if the twins will allow someone else fuck her, she even doubts if she could bring herself to be sexually attracted to another person.

"What the hell are you thinking about, you slutty bitch. Christian is my assistant and he better not have his eyes on you if he still needs it," Jacob growled when he saw that Anna was already thinking too much.

"Since, you are less busy. Why don't we get your mouth busy?" He let out, and zip down his trousers to set his hardened dick free.

Immediately his member slammed Anna's face, she felt her body react towards it instantly. Fuck,

"Suck, little slut," Jacob commanded and grabbed her head forcing it on his huge dick.

"Ohhh," Anna gagged and hummed on the piece of meat in her mouth because right now, Jacob was giving her no choice but to do this bidding and it made her body trembled in desire.

She raised her head and gave a shy smile before she leaned and dropped her head again to suck his dick while she rubbed her saliva all over it. Anna was shocked at how experienced she had been after last night.

The first person she had blowjobbed was her husband and it made her mouth hurt because she didn't find it pleasurable at all. She wished he could have stopped sooner.

But right now, she didn't want Jacob to stop at all. She wants him to fuck her mouth and call her dirty names.

At the thought of being called a whore and slut, Anna felt her pussy gushing out with juice and she rubbed her thighs together after moaning out loud.

"Daddy," she called out, gagging on Jacob's dick and it flinched at her voice.

"What is it little whore, sucking my dick makes you horny, uh?" Jacob asked, when Anna looked up at him dreamily. She looked like she wanted to be fucked raw.

And she will be, soon.

"Answer me, " Jacob slapped Anna's soft cheek and she moaned from the pain and pleasure.

"Yes, it makes me horny," Anna quickly replied, she wants him to know that so he can satisfy her. Or should she keep quiet so he can continue slapping her around like a whore? That sounds so much better.

"What makes you horny? Tell me." Jacob asked, but Anna kept quiet.

"I said what makes you horny, you whore, " Jacob asked again, but this time he was pulling Anna's head and thrusting his dick in his mouth. "Tell me, does this make you horny uh? You like being rough handled and fuck like a whore right?" He asked in a deep, baritone voice. He was completely not himself.

At the moment, he had forgotten that it was Anna that he was fucking, and Anna had forgotten that she was a girl. To Jacob she was a slut, he had picked up and wanted to fuck and to Anna herself, she was just a slut.

"Yes, I love it. I like it," Anna admitted desperately, she had totally forgotten how she had wanted to keep mute, so he could slap her around. She couldn't just keep her words in her head anymore.

Upon hearing her desperate voice, Jacob felt all senses leave his head, and he continued mouth fucking Anna until tears started coming out of hereyes..

"You like it uh? tell me how much you like it, fucking whore." Jacob said roughly and slammed his dick in her mouth again. Stunning Anna into acceptance.

She likes it, she likes it so much. Anna wanted to scream out, but because of his dick in her mouth, she couldn't voice it out. It came out as desperate murmurs which turned Jacob the fuck on.

After fucking her mouth for so long, he shoot his cum down her throat, and Anna swallowed every bit of it while looking at him like a dog who was desperate for his cum.

"Bitch," Jacob slapped her cheeks when he saw her slutty expression.

Anytime she looks at him like that, he wants to physically abuse her and make her know that it's only him and his brother that she can look at like that. They are the only ones she should submit to.

"You better don't look at another male like this, else I will fucking remove his eyes," Jacob growled, emphasizing his dominance and Anna nodded.

Not because she was agreeing but because she knew that no one can make her feel this way apart from the twins.

It didn't take much time when Christian called Jacob that he was in the driveway and Jacob smiled roughly at Anna. Finally...

"You brought everything?" He asked and Christian answered that he had brought everything he ordered.

Anna at the side who was looking confused at what he meant by everything was surprised when a tall, handsome man with broad shoulders and auburn hair came with different girls and two other men. She was totally shocked at what they were all doing here.

Apart from school, this was the first time that she will see so many people in one room.

"What are they doing here," She tugged gently at Jacob.

He smirked and replied, "You will find out,"

"Boss, this is the choker," Christian replied, glancing at the beautiful girl who was sitting beside his boss and he instantly knew what the choker was meant for. He had forgotten to add a goddamn choker to the outfit. He must be crazy.

"Hello," The girls whispered coyly at Jacob and Anna flinched in jealousy. She saw how they were exposing their breasts and also how Jacob was looking at them, she didn't know what's alluring about them. She even had bigger tits than them.

But Anna had misunderstood Jacob since he wasn't checking them out for himself, but for the men around them. He had a plan in mind.

"Christian, you can go now. Leave them with me," Jacob ordered in a deep voice and Christin quickly left. His boss fetish had no boundaries. Only God knows what he's planning on doing.

He really needs to learn a thing or two from his boss and also enjoy life while being a mafia member. But he knew he couldn't.

Immediately Christian Left, Anna looked at Jacob, wondering what he was up to and he came closer to her.

"This is for you to wear, anytime you are around me. If you fail to do that, you will be slapped and mouthfucked," Jacob asserted, tying the choker around Anna's neck as she looked up at him.

"This is a choker?" She asked innocently, and one of the girls presented snickered in contempt. Is she trying to feign innocence? Wearing that outfit and looking like a whore and she doesn't know what a choker is?

Is that even funny?

Unluckily for the girl, Jacob heard her snicker and got angry, "You, strip her," He pointed at one of the men and he went closer to the girl.

"No, wait- before that, All of you here, there's a form beside you. Take the pen and sign that everything that will happen here today is by your consent. Don't worry, you will be paid handsomely," Jacob smirked at the girls.

If they can make him look at them as he was looking at that bitch seated on the chair, they wouldn't even have to be paid handsomely before they allow him to use them.

"Now, strip them. I want my little slut here to see their damn tits," Jacob muttered, and Anna blinked at him in shock.

Is that why they are here? For her to look at them?

"Of course not, they are here to teach you how to be a proper slut." Jacob answered, as if he could read Anna's expression.

Not thinking much about it, the girls stripped and went down on their knees immediately. Almost ready for action, but Jacob laughed out loud.

"Not interesting enough." Jacob muttered, furrowing his brows and the girls raised their heads at him. "Hey you, there are chains in that locker, Go and get it and tie them up." He pointed at one of the men again, and he went to the locker.

On getting there, the man was surprised that it wasn't only chains that were there, the locker was also filled with different kinds of shotguns and rifles and so many bullets.

What kind of man keeps guns at home in a locker? The man thought, fear gripping him.

What had he gotten himself into? He only wanted to make some bucks and get pleasure while at it.

"Bring the goddamn chain," Jacob retorted when he saw that the man was taking longer than expected.

The show

"Bring the goddamn chain," Jacob retorted when he saw that the man was taking longer than expected. It was only to bring a few chains and he was using his lifetime on it.

Immediately the man brought the chains, and Jacob commanded him to tie them around the girl's body while he sat down with Anna on his lap.

"Look at them, little slut, right now you are getting tutorial's on how to be a good slut, " He whispered into Anna's ears and she couldn't help but felt sexual desires running through her veins.

Looking at the scene before her, Anna saw that the girl now had chains on their neck like bitches and they were crawling after the men who were also naked.

When she saw how the girls were being slapped around and degraded by the men, she was scared at first. She could see how much pain they were in both she also saw how much they were enjoying it because they were dripping with moisture.

She didn't know that Jacob brought her to watch a live BDSM session.

"Cat your tongues? You should moan and crave for their dicks, " Jacob threw at the girls in front of him, he felt like they weren't desperate enough.

"Little slut, can you get the vibrators in the locker?" Jacob asked Anna, who didn't know if she could even stand up at the moment owing to the fact that she was already shaking with pleasure, and also wanted to be chained down and degraded like the girls before her. This was the first time in her entire life.

"Eh?" She mumbled, incoherently.

Jacob spanked her ass and said, "get the vibrators, little slut."

Anna felt her body trembling with desire as she stood up to do his bidding. The girls watched as Jacob's eyes trailed after Anna's not-so-exposed ass, instead of their naked ones. It made them feel jealous and horny for him.

How could they be horny and desperate for these men when someone as devilishly handsome as him was in the room, they wanted him instead of these guys.

Anna brought the vibrators, and was about to drop it on the table when Jacob shook his head. "No, put it inside them," he commanded and Anna froze for a moment.

He wants her to put the vibrators inside the girls? Why?

"You know how Jackson always puts the vibrator inside you, right? You just have to put it inside them and bring the controller here." Jacob muttered as he raised his gaze at Anna, he likes seeing this look on her face.

It looks so innocent and at the same time, it looks so naughty that he felt like choking her.

With shaky hands, Anna went closer to the girls and quickly inserted the vibrators inside their exposed core. She immediately went back and sat beside Jacob. He gave her a satisfied glance after she was seated.

If someone had told her a week ago that she would be witnessing a live BDSM session, she would have looked at the person as if they were crazy. Now she was inserting vibrators into naked girls with chains on their neck.

"Switch it on, you can switch it off anytime you like," Jacob said to Anna and she widened her eyes again, stunned.

He was practically giving her the reins to the girls' pleasure. Even though she was young and inexperienced, she could tell that he was using this to know how far she could also go. If she didn't switch the vibrator off even when the girls were moaning and screaming with pleasure, he would know that she likes it and wants it this way too.

After realizing this thought, Anna couldn't help but feel her pussy clenched in anticipation. She can't wait to watch and also learn so many things from the girls.

But if she did, who would she use it on? She will be going to her husband's house after all this... Who would she practice being a slut for? She suddenly lost interest and was confused about what to do until she heard Jacob's aggressive, dominant voice.

"Switch on the fucking vibrators, " He asserted and Anna quickly switched it on,

She was still quite scared of anyone raising their hands on her but something told her that Jacob would never raise his hands on her.

And it shocked her.

She didn't know what made her trust him this much.. Not only him but also his brother.

Grabbing Anna's waist, Jacob pulled her down in front of him and said to her. "You should get on your knees too like a proper slut, don't you think?" He smirked at Anna and she looked up at him in anticipation.

Slapping her puffed cheeks, Jacob almost groaned out when she looked up at him with her gorgeous innocent eyes. Thinking about it, he felt like he should allow Jackson to hop on this.

"Watch them, " Jacob commanded, indicating the show before them and stood up to get his phone.

Clicking on facetime, he called his brother who immediately picked up since he knew that Jacob had to be doing something naughty to their new sex slave.

"Hey brother, are you busy?" Jacob asked, looking at his brother who now knew worn out even though he was still looking as handsome as hell.

"Not at the moment," He replied, and his ears instantly heard moaning voices coming from the underground. It was so loud and real that he was able to detect that it wasn't from porn and he also knew that Jacob hates watching porn.

"Brother, what are you doing to our little slut," He asked, looking at Jacob who was smirking his usual evil smirk and at the moment, he really did look like the devil that other people call him.

"Nothing, here look at her.."Jacob muttered, bringing the camera close to Anna who was still on her knees in front of Jacob.

Pulling the choker in her neck, he brought her closer to the camera and Anna looked up to see a very astonished Jackson.

Her single action of looking at him while his brother pulled the choke on her neck was even to get him hard and he knew that the image will be imprinted on his mind till the end of the day and he will never be able to focus on anything again.

"Hi, little whore," Jackson said to Anna, while he looked at the outfit she was putting on, he couldn't help but feel like she really look fucking hot and sexy in that outfit.

"Stand up, let me see your outfit," he asked, almost immediately after his last words. He wanted to see her completely.

Releasing the choker on her neck, Jacob squeezed Anna's ass and helped her to stand up on her legs but he didn't remove his hands even after helping her up.

He continue squeezing it and Anna who had initially wanted to switch off the vibrator remote in her hands mistakenly pressed on the highest and the girls started moaning out loud in pleasure while the men fucked them fuck them from the back.

Looking at Anna's complete outfit and how she looked so sexy in it, Jackson knew that he needed to be where she was because he can't help but want to fuck her.

"You are missing out, brother," Jacob muttered in a bemused tone and told Anna to get back on her knees. That was when Anna saw that the remote was on the highest and her eyes immediately went to the girls before her.

At the moment, they were being fucked in their asses and they were looking as if they couldn't get enough while the men pulled chains on their necks. It looked strangely hot and satisfying to Anna and she could feel that she was seeing herself in place of them, with Jacob and Jackson filling holes with their dicks.

No, Anna, stop thinking like this! You are married, she reminded herself but quickly forgot it when Jacob pulled the choker on her neck again.

"Oh daddy, please fuck my ass hole," One of the girls' moaned out when she saw Jacob pulling Anna's neck. In her dirty mind, she imagined that she was being pulled and fucked by Jacob, instead of the man at her back.

"That's it!" Jacob let out an excited tone. "That's how they should scream and shout for the men filling your cunts and take it like the obedient whore you are." His rough voice instantly made Anna wet. "Fuck them, till they scream and every one of you will be paid double." Jacob added.

He wasn't interested in their moans or the girls who were looking at him as if they wanted him instead, what he was interested in was for Anna to see how the girls were hungry for their master's dicks.

Immediately going into role play, the men started hitting the girls ass and speaking to them in a harsh tone as they slipped in and out of them. "Spread your fucking legs, and arch your back you fucking slut," the man who had went to bring the chains earlier said to the girl he was fucking and he instantly slapped her ass cheeks as he thrusted into her with full force.

"Oh yes, daddy.. ahhh," The girl moaned out as she looked at Jacob who was stuffing his dick inside Anna's open mouth.

"Ouuu," Anna gagged, she was on her knees and Jacob was pulling the choker and was also fucking her mouth with his dick. Sexual desires spread through her from her hair down to her core, and she could see that her panties were already drenched with her pussy juice.

Squeezing her legs as she had seen one of the girls do earlier, Anna was able to withstand the pleasure until Jacob slapped her cheeks. She instantly felt herself unable to stop moaning and she moaned out while she choked on his dick.

Upon hearing her voice, the men instantly turned their eyes to look at her as they couldn't believe that she could sound so good, instantly hardened and horny all over again they started thrusting faster and harder into the girls push as they pretended that they were fucking Anna instead.

Immediately Jacob saw them looking at Anna, his mood instantly changed.

Jacob's anger

"Leave!" He yelled at them in a strong, powerful voice and the men who were about to cum quickly pulled out when they saw Jacob's expression. If expression could kill, they would have died with the way Jacob stared at them.

Picking his phone up, he dialed Christian's number. "Come and pick them up in ten minutes, else it will be their bodies you will be retrieving," Jacob yelled on the phone at his assistant.

Where the fuck did Christian find hungry ass men that don't understand the rule! How dare they look at his pet.

Not waiting for ten minutes before they were picked up, the men immediately started picking up whatever belonged to them and attempted to leave until they found out that the door was locked, and they stared at it with a shocked expression.

The man who had seen the various kinds of guns that Jacob had stacked in his drawer was visibly shaking and he was the most frightened one out of the two men. The other one wasn't any better, he was shaking but it wasn't as visible as the first man.

The girls were the worst, they still had a working vibrator in their pussies and they were tired. No matter how they tried to leave, they couldn't as the pleasure was too much for them to handle and they couldn't stop moaning loudly.

Anna, who was still on her knees, was totally shocked and confused as to why the live show had abruptly stopped. She looked up at Jacob in confusion and felt a wave of fear shoot through her. This was the first time she would see him as angry as this.

But what did she know? She just met him and his brother and apart from their last names and the fact that Jackson works in an office, she didn't know anything about them.

Seeing Anna glancing at him, Jacb tried to flash her a smirk, but it came out as evil as always which almost made Anna monetarily shift a bit from him.

Not able to accept how scared she was looking at him, Jacob got angrier at the men and the girl's moaning was also making him angry.

"Untie those bitches and shut their fuxking mouths with something," he yelled to the men angrily and his voice enveloped the whole.

Running to do his bidding, His aura and voice was so strong that the men almost fell on their knees with fears and frightening faces. Even the girls had momentarily stopped moaning because Anna had picked up the vibrator remotes and turned it off thinking that it was the girls voices that was making Jacob angry.

It didn't take up to ten minutes when Christian pulled up in the vacation house driveway in total dismay and confusion. He couldn't stop wondering what the men and the girls he picked had done to get his boss angry.

His Boss wasn't that short tempered, unless the offense was too big. He will just smirk his usual evil smirk as he plans the person murder. So he was really short of words and brain on what could have possibly happened.

Thinking about how he still had to go back to the port to check the goods they will be delivering tomorrow made him swear under his breath.

Damn those inexperienced bitches and dogs.

Inserting the key to the vacation house, he was cursing in his way until he reached where Jacob was with the people he had brought.

Unlocking the room, he went inside to see an angry Jacob and also the men shivering from the fear and the naked women. Looking at the scenes, he could see that it was the men that offended Jacob and they had affected the girls with their stupidness.

Upon seeing that the door was open, the men didn't wait for Christain to say a word before rushing out of the room and he stared at them in surprise.

For them to be still alive before he got there meant his boss wasn't interested in killing them because he knew how Jacob operates. His decisions are always fast and effective within two minutes. If he had wanted them dead, he wouldn't have even called him.

"Boss..." Christian let out slowly as he raised his eyes up to look at Jacob, but he couldn't stand the oppressive aura in it so he quickly looked down.

Eww, why is he so damn angry.

Did the men asked to fuck his pet or what? Christian thought as he glanced at the latest pet of his Boss after a few months of abstinence, and he could see that she was also scared.

But Christian would never have thought that the men weren't even brazen enough to ask that, they had just stared at Anna a little bit too much and they were caught by Jacob which was what resulted in Jacob's anger.

"Pay them their money and make sure they keep their mouths shut. If not, you know what to do." Jacob let out in a mild voice. But when his eyes shifted to the girls and how they were looking at him, he got angry again.

"Take these bitches with you and the fucking vibrators. I don't want to see any traces that they were once here." Jacob added, in a pitch voice.

Normally, he felt like he shouldn't be that angry over them looking at his pet, but he didn't know what had sparked in him that made him so angry when he saw them looking at Anna.

He was so angry that he wanted to shoot them died, but he remembered how Anna had gotten frightened and terrified just by Jackson yelling at her, he was sure that she might faint if he shot them right before her.

That was why he didn't do anything to them before Christian arrived and he had kept his anger in him.

"Yes Boss, " Christain replied and motioned for the girls to quickly grab whatever belonged to them and leave when Jacob was still calm and they did exactly what he had said.

Seeing that they had left, Jacob picked up the scared and shaky Anna and carried her to the other room while Christian cleaned up the large sitting room.

After placing her gently on the bed, Jacob saw that she was still shaking and she wasn't even willing to look at him and he felt his anger rising again. He wished he had shot the men's legs or arms to get rid of his anger while they were still around because at the moment he was so angry and he didn't have anyone to let it out on.

"Look at me, " He said to Anna, trying to sound as calm as possible, but Anna was too scared to look at him.

She closed her eyes and shivered on the bed. She was so scared. She had thought he was going to hit her, she actually thought he was going to hurt her.

Seeing her breaths coming more rapidly and quickly, Jacob could sense that she was crying. Using his hands to forcibly hold her chin, he looked at her and saw that she had closed her eyes and there were tears falling on her cheeks.

"Stop crying and open your eyes, goddamnit, " He wanted to yell out but he cautioned himself, and tightened his hand in a blow.

Slowly fluttering her eyes opened, Anna looked up at Jacob and she saw the worry in his eyes and she was shocked for a moment. He was angry and furious earlier, he was yelling and he looked so fierce.

How come he was now looking at her with worry and anxiety, wasn't he gonna hit her?

Wasn't he going to punish her like how her father always did?

"Why are you crying? I didn't yell at you, " Jacob said defensively. He had actually cautioned his action when he was angry earlier. He had even smiled at her or didn't she see it?

"You didn't, " Anna replied in a low voice, he hadn't actually yelled at her but he was angry and she had thought that he would hit her.

She was scared, that's all.

"So why are you crying? You are still shaking." Jacob asserted, seeing that she was still visibly shaking.

"I... was.. I was scared that you would hit me, " Anna let out slowly in a low tone and a few tears fell off her cheeks as she remembered how angry Jacob was a few minutes ago.

"Hit you? I will never hit you, sweet slut, unless we are in the bedroom and you want me to give you pleasure. I won't ever raise my hands on you, " Jacob said to Anna in a clear voice and he meant it.

Looking at his eyes, Anna knew that he was telling the truth and she found out that she believed him. She actually believes him.

Jacob leaned forward and gently learned to kiss her plum lips, when he saw that she had calmed down a little bit. Anna moaned softly immediately she felt his hard lips on hers. She hated and liked how she quickly reacted to his, and also his brother's touch anytime they touched her.

They made her feel like a jelly and she wants to melt any time they touch her. Hearing her low seductive voice, Jacob tore the tiny skirt she was putting on along with her panties and dipped a hand inside her wet core.

He was about to start thrusting his finger in and out of her pussy when he heard the door open, and he groaned out while he turned his back to look at the intruder who dared to walk on him without knocking.

Jackson is back

He was about to start thrusting his finger in and out of Anna's p*ssy when he heard the door open, and he groaned out while he turned his back to look at the intruder who dared to walk on him without knocking.

He turned his head to see his twin brother, Jackson in front of the door, with the first two buttons on his shirt loosened, and his suit in his left hand, while he held his briefcase in the other hand.

It was Anna that first spoke out. "Jackson, you are back?" She muttered, in a surprise tone because she had just seen him a few minutes ago on Facetime.

"Yes, I couldn't resist that wet ass pussy that much." Jackson retorted as a matter of fact. He was surprised that Jacob was also done with his mini show.

Considering how he had rushed things from work, and how he had taken his private jet instead, he was hoping he would meet the show and Anna is a choker. He really wanted to see her in that little skirt and choker on her neck, she looked so hot on the videos that he almost masturbated in his office for the first time.

"I thought as much," Jacob scoffed and rolled his eyes at his brother.

Anna didn't know what to say though, she didn't know if she should encourage it or not. But seeing Jackson in a business suit and briefcase turned her on and she almost got her pants wet again.

"What's that expression on your face, Little slut?" It was Jacob that first saw Anna's face filled with lust because he was right beside her and his brother quickly caught on.

"Guess, she missed her second daddy, don't you Anna?" Jackson smirked at her and came closer to the bed.

Not able to resist his sexual appeal, she replied shyly, "Yes,"

"Yes what?" Jackson asked,

"Yes, I miss my second daddy, " Anna replied exactly how Jackson wanted her to say it, and he smiled dangerously at her.

"Obedient, now uh?" he let out, touching the Vee of her lap and Anna bit her inner mouth in resistance. She didn't want to give in so soon.

"Why is she still so shy?" Jacob asked, unable to discern how Anna still managed to be so innocent even after they've fucked her so many times already..

"Probably because we have not entered her at the same time, " His brother replied, putting his fingers inside Anna's mouth and dipping it in her throat. Anna coated his fingers with her saliva and gently sucked on it which made Jackson groan inwardly.

Maybe she's not so shy after all.

"Is that what you want, little sl*t? Do you want my brother and me to f*ck you at the same time? Do want us to fuck your asshole and pussy at the same time?" he asked, pulling Anna's choker with a bit of force and she moaned out softly

Maybe she's not so shy after all.

When he says it like that, it made her really want to beg for it.

She didn't know why she yearned to have them at the same time. But that was exactly what she was feeling right at the moment. Slowly nodding her head, Anna replied, "Yes, I want, "

"You see, I knew she's just a shy slut." Jackson said to his brother and raised his hand to squeeze Anna's breasts that were already spilling out from the short blouse she was putting on.

"Come here, come and suck daddy." Jackson pulled Anna's choker and gently dragged her closer to him. As she crawled towards him, she had her ass up, and wet exposed to Jacob's eyes, he gulped when he saw how she was dripping with pussy juice.

"What made you so wet?" Jacob asked, moving closer to her as her before he dipped a finger inside her.

Anna, who already had her hands on Jackson's dick realized the position she was in and blushed hard. She hadn't really done that intentionally, she just wanted to do what his brother said.

Seeing that she didn't answer, Jacob added another digit and Anna moaned on Jackson's dick. She wasn't expecting him to continue but he added another finger. "I was thinking about having you guys inside me, " she confessed slowly in a low voice, but because Jackson was closer to her, he heard her loud and clear.

Grabbing her head, he choked her with his dick because that was all he wanted to do at that time. "When you talk like that, you make me crazy, " Jackson groaned as he felt her deep throat.

"She's a wild little thing, " His brother replied, spanking Anna's ass roughly and squeezing it. He also can't wait to hear her moans when she has them inside her. He wants to watch her hungrily take them and ask for more.

He started thrusting his fingers inside her as she sucked his brother's dick.

"Fuck." Jacob groaned inwardly.

He couldn't wait to be inside her, Jacob thought and he immediately acted on by removing his trousers and briefs. Gently nudging her legs apart, He inserted his dick inside her and she moaned suddenly in pleasure and irresistible desire.

Stroking inside her, Jacob maintained a steady rhythm until Anna started moaning out loudly in lust and desire. It made him want to knead her faster and deeper.

"Ahh, " she groaned in pleasure as Jackson's dick fell off her mouth.

"Scream louder, bitch" Jacob said to Anna as he spanked her ass over and over again. She felt pain and pleasure at the same time as her legs trembled slightly. She really wants to scream out, but she also wants to continue getting spanked like their little slut.

While she was getting slutted out by his brother, Jackson also had his dick deep inside her mouth as he held her hair in his hand.

The pleasure was overwhelming and oppressive to Anna's lustful pussy as it was pouring out juices and it was coating Jacob's hard dick, it made his thrusts faster and sloppy.

Groaning out, Jacob dick hardened and he lost his will power as he started thrusting harder and faster touching her G-spot with each stroke.

"Ahh, " Anna cried out again as the sexual frictions overwhelmed her.. She couldn't stop herself from pouring outside as Jacob fucked her pussy. She could feel her climax coming, but it seemed so far and her body wanted to attain it faster because of the sexual cravings she was feeling deep inside her core.

"Harder, please." She moaned.

A few minutes later, Anna felt climax wash over her and she groaned out as Jackson butter in her mouth, and his brother nutted in her pussy.

"Shit, " Jacob groaned as he felt her pussy walls tighten around him, milking out his cum. "Fucking slut, " He grunted, spanking her hard on her ass cheeks.

Looking at her sexy and alluring face, Jackson felt like smashed her face too. He loves when she looks like that, always makes him want to dominate and slap her around.

"Here, come here," Jackson said to Anna and gently unhooked the choker on her neck while slapping her puffy cheeks.

"You look so good right now, I want to fuck your mouth again," He told Anna and he rub her hardened nipple which was now rubbing against his chest.

"I love that view, " Jacob asserted, looking at Anna's ass in the air until his phone interrupted their sexual activities.

Picking up his phone, Christian's voice was heard on the other line. "Boss, the goods arrived. But you might need to come instantly. There's a problem with the port."

"Fine, I will be there in 30." Jacob answered in a deep powerful voice, he had switched to the mafia boss that he was. Who could possibly stop his men from offloading?

Seeing his brother's expression, Jackson knew that he was about to have Anna to himself. "Take my jet, it's in the hangar. " He volunteered.'

"You came in a jet?" Anna asked in shock. No wonder he got here so fast.

"Yeah, I told you I couldn't resist that wet ass pussy, " Jackson replied with a half-smile, and Anna blushed hard.

Jacob quickly dressed up and prepared to leave for the port. "I will be back soon," He said to Anna, blowing her a kiss before he left the room for business.

After his brother, Jackson shifted his attention to Anna and covered her body with his firm ones and he raised her legs to see her wet pussy glistening. Aroused by the tempting view, he plunged a finger inside her. When he brought it out, it was drenched with Anna's juice.

Jackson smiled, and inserted it in her mouth. "Taste yourself, little slut."

Blinking at him, Anna sucked his finger and licked it all off as she had seen the girls do early. She had noticed that the men actually like it while the girls suck on their fingers. She would rather suck on his dick though, she likes his big meat in her mouth.

"Shit," Jackson groaned and slapped Anna's puffy cheeks. "Oh, so you learn how to be a slut already uh?" He muttered as he inserted his fingers in her pussy again.

And here he was wondering why he was hearing girls moaning in the face time, Jacob must have brought sluts over to tutor her.

"What else did you learn today, little whore? Mind showing daddy?" Jackson asked in a deep, dangerous voice.

Blinking her eyes in surprise, Anna didn't know that she would be caught so easily and she flushed straight to her ears. She remembered how the girls were on chains and couldn't do anything other than receiving all the strokes and the thrusts from the men that had been fucking them and she felt her pussy tighten again in pleasure.

Fucking her husband's supposed Boss

"What? You don't want to tell daddy what you learned today, uhn?" Jackson asked, flickering his thumb around Anna's clit while watching her moan in satisfaction.

"I...can't, " Anna replied, between moans and Jackson smirked at her.

"You don't have to tell, you can show me, " He asserted as he flipped her on her knees. "They were on their knees, right? Sucking like whores? Uh?" Jackson added as he grabbed Anna's cheeks and she nodded.

"Well, you should do the same. Don't you think so?" He asked the shy, but slutty Anna, who was already feeling the dampness of her pussy.

Loosening Jackson's trousers and brief, Anna drew them down gently as her hands shake from aspiration and sexual desires. She knows the next action that will come after Jackson's dick is undone from its cage. She knew that she was about to get fucked and used again as she like.

Gently wrapping her tiny, fragile hands on Jackson's dick, Anna's eyes widened in shock when she saw how hard and swollen it was even though she hadn't even started sucking it.

"What? This is not your first time sucking it, why are you hesitating?" Jackson asked, when he saw the look of resistance in Anna's eyes but unknown to him, she was just wondering how it became so big without any action rather than what Jackson had thought.

"It's big and hard," Anna managed to let out before Jackson forced his dick inside her warm and wet mouth, while Anna let her saliva coat around it willingly. Even though it was big, it felt so meaty in her mouth and made her feel so sexy.

Jackson held Anna's hair as he plunged into her mouth, in a steady rhythm before going faster and harder while Anna moaned and groaned wildly like a whore because of the penetrating and hard thrust.

"Shut up bitch, take the cock like the slut you are, " Jackson remarked, irritated when Anna didn't stop groaning.

Jackson's dick was widening her mouth, but she was loving it because he was making her feel used and whorish. She loves the feeling so much that she can stop herself from moaning out but Jackson wants her to take it like a good girl.

"Do you like Daddy's dick?" Jackson asked, holding Anna's soft hands with one hand and her hair with another hand. Immediately he saw her nod, he threw her on the bed and started choking her with his dick while pinning her hands above her head.

"Since you like it so much, then I will treat you like the whore you are, "Jackson said to Anna, and she managed to nod her approval before she felt him fill her whole mouth again.

After gagging and choking, Jackson spreads Anna's legs and beats his dick on her pussy several times, making her wet, ready, and anticipating his huge dick before thrusting it widely inside her in a swift and hard thrust.

"Oh my..." Anna couldn't complete her words before Jackson added several thrusts to accompany the first one. Moans and groans filled the room while sweat and hot breathes were shared between Anna and Jackson.

It was more than an hour before Jackson finally ejaculated on Anna's huge and sizable breasts and watched it stream down her tummy.

"You are so sexy, " he breathed out as he looked at how desirable Anna was at the moment. Her eyelids were only closing and her mouth was slightly agape from extinct orgasm.

"You too, " Anna complimented, taking in Jacksons manly features, his big and muscular shoulder, and biceps, his abs, and also his handsome face.

"Do you want to stay here or should we go back to the mansion?" Jackson asked Anna as he picked her up from the bed to take a shower.

"To the mansion, " Anna answered, she was a person of short words. She had slowly mastered the behavior after years of being maltreated and beaten by her own father. She can't even bring herself to say everything she wants to say. She always felt like the more she talks, the higher the possibility of people finding fault in it.

"Why? You don't like it here?" Jackson asked, turning on the shower and letting the water flow on Anna's tummy and breasts to watch away from his cum on her body.

"Aren't you leaving for work?" Anna answered, giving him a reason. But not the actual reason why she didn't want to stay at the vacation house.

"Yeah, you are right. I have to leave for work, also I can't leave you here, " Jackson nodded after listening to Anna.

After the shower, he wrapped Anna in one of Jacob's shirts since they were in his home and the only dress his stupid brother brought for Anna was the slutty dress which wasn't comfortable to wear anymore.

"We should leave early if we are going to the mansion, I have to call Zane, " Jackson said to Anna before taking his phone from his suit to make a call.

On his departure, his leg hit the briefcase he brought with him when he came in and its contents spilled on the floor. Seeing the mess, Anna stood up from the bed and went closer to the briefcase to pack the documents inside the briefcase.

While she was packing it, she saw a vaguely familiar name on a document, but before she could see it clearly, Jackson came back into the room.

"It fell?" He asked, indicating the briefcase and she nodded.

"Zane will be here soon, what did you want to eat?" He asked, but Anna doesn't feel like buying a takeout. She declined and asked if there were any foodstuffs.

"I'm sure, you'd only find raw meats and a few vegetables in the kitchen. That's precisely what Jacob eats." Jackson replied with a shrug. He knew how much his twin brother loves steaks. "Are you sure you don't want to order pizza, ice cream, or something?" he added before Anna left the room.

"No, I will be done in a few minutes, " Anna answered, as she left the room. Leaving Jackson to sort out the documents and the files that had fallen earlier.

Packing the documents, Jackson also saw a familiar name but he didn't put his mind to it before filling it up inside the briefcase again. While packing, he made a mental tone to ask Paige, his secretary about the new contractors he had asked her to look for and if the documents were from them.

It didn't take up to fifteen minutes when Anna came outside the kitchen with two plates of French steaks and fries. The combination was far better than what Jacob used to force his brother to eat.

"Wow, this looks tasty, " Jackson complement with a smile tugging on his lips as he eyes Anna and the plate. At the moment, one wouldn't be able to say if he meant the food or the chef who made the food.

"Where do you learn to cook like this?" Jackson asked, in a rough contended voice after downing the steaks with red wine. He felt like this was the best French steaks and fries he had ever tried.

Excitedly Anna replied, "At home when I was..." she couldn't complete her words when she realized that there's no way she can tell him about how she had mastered the art of cooking without telling him how she had to drop out of school.

"When you were what?" Jackson asked, raising an eyebrow at Anna but she became quiet again and used the excuse of packing the dishes to avoid Jackson's questions.

Before she got back to the sitting room, Zane already arrived and they instantly left for the mansion. All the way, Anna's mind was calculating how she had to leave Michealson's brothers tomorrow because she had to go back to her husband's house.

Jackson noticed her absent-mindedness but he didn't point it out as he was also thinking about what she couldn't bring herself to say before Zane came.

'The marks on her body, is it from her childhood? Is it inflicted by her parents? Or by her new husband?' Jackson thought deeply as they reached the mansion.

"Should I help you with her?" Zane asked, when he saw that his boss was trying to carry the lady even with his briefcase and suit.

"No, " Jackson muttered in a dominant and possessive voice.

"Oh, the briefcase then, " Zane quickly understood his stance before Jackson handed him the briefcase and they both went inside the mansion with Anna carried gently by Jackson.

The next morning when Anna woke up, she couldn't find any traces of Jackson because she woke up pretty late and it was already past 9 am. Struggling to stretch her tiny body, Anna's eyes flickered at the familiar briefcase she had seen last night and saw that Jackson must have forgotten or he might not have left for work yet.

Instantly going through the documents again, Anna saw the document she had seen earlier last night and thought it was familiar. It was a document with her husband's name on it.

Anna left the twins

Widening her eyes in shock, Anna went through the documents and saw that her husband had applied as a contractor for a new project that Jackson's company had issued out.

What the hell!!

Her husband will soon be working under the Jackson's company and he will be her husband's boss.

'Does that mean that she had fucked her husband's potential employer?' Anna's eyes momentarily took a few steps back in shock as she dropped the documents on the floor.

She had to leave! Immediately!

Anna said to herself as she grabbed whatever belonged to her, her phones, bag, and everything before hurriedly leaving the mansion. She didn't even book an Uber before she left, she opted for a taxi and gave her house address.

On her way back home, she deleted her profile and also her Tumblr in panic. The terror and fear she felt was enough to get her shaking and shattering.

"Are you okay, Miss?" The taxi driver asked but Anna didn't reply because she was busy deleting anytime that can make her remember the twins or can make the twin trace her.

Feeling glad that she has actually come on her own to their mansion and they don't have her house address, Anna felt relief washed through her. She believed that if they can't find her on Tumblr and also social media, they will let her be.

She was a married woman and they are going to be her husband's boss. She knew that whatever adultery she had committed had to stop!

'Are you sure you can forget about the twins?' A tiny voice asked Anna but she instantly waved it off.

She had to!

Even though she doesn't want to, she had to forget about the twins because she's married.

Getting to her husband's mansion, Anna saw that her husband hadn't arrived yet and the car was still intact, exactly how she had left it before going to The Michealson's brothers mansion. She knew that she should feel ashamed and embarrassed for her adulterous actions, but her body was doing the opposite.

Instead of feeling embarrassed, it was twitching and shuddering from pleasure as she remembered the twins and how they had fucked and spoiled her.

When Anna got inside her husband's mansion, the familiar interior designs and the setting forced her to remember her status as a wedded woman and also the terms of the marriage. To give birth to children for her husband.

It made her remember that she was just a producing machine and an exchange for her father's huge and unpaid debts which instantly sobered her up.

After her realization, Anna decided to completely forget everything about the twins, the sexual attraction, their manliness, their handsomeness and also how they gently care for her and baths her after fucking her into oblivious.

She knew that she will never experience such with her husband but she felt complete as she had once known what wonderful sex could be. Now the puzzle was how to tell her husband that she wasn't a virgin anymore.

After several thoughts, Anna concluded that she would just tell him that she had used a dildo on herself because she felt horny and needy. Even though she knew that her husband might not believe her, she also knew that she had no other options apart from this since she was supposed to be a virgin.

Jackson, who had accidentally taken another briefcase instead of the one Zane brought, wasn't aware of the mistake until he wanted to check some documents for that day's meeting.

After realizing his mistakes, he called Zane to bring the briefcase since he had no time to go back to the mansion. It was almost up to an hour before Zane finally came with the briefcase in his hands but with a slight frown on his face.

He didn't know whether to tell his boss that he couldn't find the lady again but he later dismissed it since he thought that she must be left to get something. Jackson also doesn't ask anything about Anna because he had thought that she would be home, waiting for him to come back.

Running through the documents, Jackson passed it all to Paige after assigning the contractor he had chosen, with the name of James Riley. He saw that the man had more years of experience and also a good reference. So he picked him instead of the rest before leaving his office to discuss it with his executives.

That was Jackson's method, he made decisions on his own and before discussing it with his executives because he was the boss and not a joint owner.

"But do you think Mr. Riley is good for the job?" One of the executives asked Jackson and he raised his eyes up at him with a penetrating look.

"Do you have better suggestions?" he asked in a cold, rough voice which instantly put the exclusive in his place. He regretted ever speaking up in the first place. He didn't understand why Jackson was discussing his decisions with them after making up his mind on who to give the contract to.

Seeing that the man already kept his mouth shut, Jackson glanced at everyone in the conference with cold eyes, daring anyone to talk or even breathe wrongly.

"Since we all agreed, you should ask Paige for the documented application of Mr. Riley and also discuss the contract with the lawyer.

Make sure you tell him that I want the building within six- months," Jackson retorted before leaving the conference room in bold strides and unmatched confidence.

"Such a young bully, " One of the eldest executives mouthed immediately Jackson left and the rest nodded their head in approval.

"I'm damn sure that he doesn't even know who Mr. Riley was. I wanted to recommend Mr. Danish, do you remember him? He's the man who I said came to my house a few weeks ago because of the contract," The executive who had spoken before, about whether Mr. Riley was a good contractor for the job.

"Well, I guess you should have collected the bribe then because our boss already chose who he wants and he's not Mr. Danish." His colleague replied as a matter of fact, and the other frowned....

In the port, Jacob had settled all the rightful agencies after finding out that it wasn't another gang that was delaying his goods but the government.

"Boss, how long do we have to pay the ports?" Christian asked in an irritated voice.

"As long as we are still running a mob, we have to give what belongs to Caesar, to Caesar." Jacob answered after assuring that all his goods were safe.

"But they really went far this time, they are not supposed to withhold the goods." Christian argued with a frown as he remembered how the port guards had almost found out the goods they had shipped.

"Did they check the goods?" Jacob asked in a cold, hard voice.

"No, boss, "

"Well then, there's no reason to dispose of them. Just leave them alone for now, if it happens again, you can just dispose of them off, " Jacob said to Christian as a bit of anger flickered on his eyes.

He wasn't angry about the fact that they had withheld the goods, he was angrier that he had to leave Anna and come to just settle stupid goddamn port guards.

"Yes, Sir." Christian answered as they left the port.

"Tell the brothers that we will be leaving for Italy in two days, I need to meet up with the prince. We have new deals, " Jacob told Christian again after he remembered the unfinished business he had with the Italian second prince.

"But Boss, you have to leave for the states tomorrow, how do you plan on getting to Italy in the next two days?" Christian asked, confused about his Boss' change of plan.

"Cancel it. Let whoever wants to see me wait. I have to go back to the vacation house, " Jacob replied in a short and cold voice.

"Okay boss, " Christian replied and left for the Mafia house while Jacob entered his latest Audi and drove to the vacation house.

When he got there, he saw the absence of Anna and he instantly frowned before taking his phone to call his twin brother.

"Where's the little slut?" Jacob asked,

"Took her back to the mansion, she can't stay alone there while waiting for you, " Jackson replied his brother and Jacon instantly hung up before leaving the vacation house again in his Audi to the mansion that he shares with his brother.

On his way to the mansion, he felt a dreadful feeling in his heart, but he kept ignoring it because he felt like there shouldn't be anything wrong until he got inside the mansion and didn't see any traces of Anna again.

"She's not here," Jacob said to his brother again on the phone, but this time with fierce coldness.

Not an update!!!!!!!

Hi guys, long time no smut books. But not to worry, I'm currently working on a new work! It's a short erotica book, and I've attached the blurb as image. KINDLY CHECK IT OUT

Here is an excerpt of the book (Need y'all suggestion for book title) *********************************I knew what I was here for, it wasn't my first time. I am not proud of it, but I've come to enjoy it. Every bit of it.

Why?

Because I have a humiliation kink- I enjoyed being fucked and dragged around.

"I'm sorry, master." I quickly dropped my gaze, but the effect of his attractiveness was already sipping down my panties. Wetting my panties and making me delirious from irresistible cravings.

"Sorry?" He gave a throaty laugh at my words before he pulled my hair and roughly pulled my tiny body towards him. "In this room, when you apologize, you apologize with your cunt."

His words were loud and clear as they traveled onto my ears but as my body met with his, my brain went blank, and I felt my pussy clenched from expectations of what to come.

"I will apologize anyhow you want me to, master," I begged.

His stronghold on my head was affecting my senses yet I want him to be rougher. I've heard lots of tales about the only prince of Raevarno, and I've craved him ever since I learned that he was a masochist.

He was just the right man that I needed to satisfy my abomination kinks.

"Filthy whore." He yelled at me before he pushed me down before him. His face was enshrouded with anger. Aside from making eye contact with him, I couldn't recall what I had done that made him so mad.

"Do you look like men like that and expected not to be fucked like a bitch?" Prince Alaric grabbed the red sexy nightmare I've been made to wear and tear it open, revealing my voluptuous breast to his sharp eyes.

Aside from him being angry, I could sense the arousal in his voice. I couldn't believe it. I had managed to arouse Prince Alaric. It was like a dream came through. This realization made me horny, and edgy. Moaning inwardly, I tried to rub my thighs together to reduce the ache growing beneath my core, but his sharp eyes caught my action, and he slapped my thighs open.

"If you close your legs again, I will make sure to tie you up." He threatened coldly, and I gulped in fright and arousal. I've never been tied up.

All my previous masters loved seeing me beg for their cocks. Especially the old brawny ones with little unsatisfying cocks.

"Look how wet you are." Prince Alaric murmured as he lifted one of my thighs and wrapped it around him. Bringing him closer to the V of my thighs. I felt my pussy clenched at the little contact, and I looked down to see him stroking my panties.

His lips were curled now curled in amusement but I was under torture. His torture, because I knew he had to know what he was doing to me. He couldn't just wrap my leg around him, teasing my entrance, and expect me to lay still right?

As if listening to my thoughts, he moved his hands away from my wet panties and brought them to my breasts. He gave each of them a slap that got them red in an instant. I groaned from the pain, and he laughed.

"You like it, don't you?" He asked, and I nodded obediently. He was right.

"Yes, master. I like it." I admitted.

An excerpt from season 3

"These are the only items that were delivered?" Jacob sneered after inspecting a few boxes. He was raging with frustration and anger. He hadn't believed that the Italian prince would go as far as to mess with his other deliveries just because he hadn't kept to his promise to leave for Italy after they delivered the guns.

"The last one didn't get delivered." His closest subordinate after Christian disclosed as he clenched his fist.

"Send one of these to Christian's house. He is to keep a box and give one of the guns to Rhoda." Jacob ordered before dismissing him.

His father hadn't said the reason for this urgent meeting but he had also been in the game for so long. He must have heard about everything and he probably wants to discuss that, or something else. Jacob couldn't be certain about what his father had wanted to discuss but he was sure that London was not safe for Rhoda. Birmingham was currently the safest place for her, but she cannot leave without protection.

"Schedule another meeting with the Italian Prince. I will meet up with him on Monday." Jacob added before dispersing his men and leaving for the VIP section.

When he got there, he was surprised to see that Jackson and Anna had left. He was about to call Jackson when he saw that he had missed his call and his texts. 'Meet us at the suite'

Once he received his twin brother's texts, Jacob didn't hesitate for a second before he left for the next building, which is Sodom Hotel, through the secret passage.

When he got inside the private VIP suite meant for him and his brother, he was surprised to see Anna naked and cuffed to the bed

"This- I wasn't expecting to see this." His voice traveled to Anna's ears before she raised her head to see him. "Fuck." His eyes trailed all over Anna's skin which shone bright with the light. He was so tempted to pour wine on her body and lick it off.

"She wanted to be cuffed again," Jackson told his brother and Jacob chuckled before he stood before Anna.

"You want us to continue from where we stopped in the pleasure room, don't you?" He asked Anna before his eyes trailed down at her body again.

Squeezing her soft huge breasts, he twirled her hardened nipples under his thumbs. Anna moaned out from pain and pleasure.

"Ah.."

Jackson in turn shoved his hand into her mouth and choked her with it. "You are supposed to answer, not moan, slut."

"Yes, I...want, please." Anna could hardly reply with Jackson's fish in her mouth. She hadn't thought much about it when Jackson had asked her what to do about her longing, and she had just said the first thing in her mind.

But now, she realized that her mind knew her body better than herself. She was their slut, their sex toy, and sex slave, and she would be anything for them as long as they want her and treat her like they'd always done.

If this was the only relationship they could have, she will be less disappointed if they later find out about her dirty past.

Deciding to enjoy every bit of what they could give her until then, Anna raised her head at the twins again and slowly opened her legs, so they could see how wet she was.

Jacob and Jackson groaned when they saw her glistening pussy. They undressed almost immediately and joined her on the bed. Not warning her, Jacob leaned forward to take one of her nipples in his mouth while his brother poke his dick into her wet entrance.

He didn't tease her or linger before he thrust into her in one swift thrust. Making Anna cry out from the aggressive thrust. Receiving pleasure from Jackson and his brother while her hands were tied to the bed was driving Anna crazy. Sizzling sensations build and disperse in her before she could reach the peak.

Jacob now had his dick in Anna's warm mouth but it wasn't still enough for Anna. Her asshole was throbbing and aching to be fucked too. She wanted them to fuck her at the same time in her holes.

Excerpts that I can't wait to show y'all

Hey guys, check on the cover, and let me know what you think about it! I'm publishing the book for free as my Christmas gift to y'all

This excerpt for season 3 >>>>

"Then we should make sure she gets both creams as much as she wants."

Jacob also agreed with his brother and brought out his phone to place an order at his favorite restaurant, and some ice cream for Anna at Amirrino.

"You remember her favorite flavor?" Jackson raised a surprised brow at Jacob. He couldn't believe that indifferent twin brother also remembered that tiny bit of information about Anna.

"Of course, I do." Jacob smirked, his eyes showing a tenderness. " I also know that she doesn't seem to eat bacon. Perhaps, she doesn't like pork." He shrugged his shoulders casually before grabbing a cigarette to smoke, "I think she loves steaks like me."

"How did you know she didn't like Bacon but loves steak?" Jackson chuckled faintly. In his kitchen, he probably only had milk and some basic ingredients. If Anna loves Bacon, they wouldn't know since Jacob always adds steaks to his diet.

Jacob took a drag and puffed it into the air before a tiny smile appeared on his lips. His smile was almost identical to his evil smirk, but it has a freshness to it like he was thinking about something remarkable as he smokes.

"You are in love with her too, right?" Jackson had to ask his brother because he was also feeling this way. In the beginning, he was only attracted to her stunning body and her eagerness to try out any sexual kinks that they wants, and also how she was always wet and ready for them. But slowly, he became possessive of her, even though they clearly knew she was married.

"Yes, I mean.. I don't even know when it started. At first, she was just like any other sex slave to me. Then, I got intrigued by her innocence, so I yearned to violate it. I wanted her to crave and think of having her holes filled with our cocks every time. I wanted to degrade her while pleasuring her more than anyone, so she could know that she was meant for us only. But anytime she raised her head to look at me, I want to do more than fuck her. I want to love her, punish her, take her out on dates, have her carry our kids, and only have her in our lives."

Jackson could only stare with his mouth agape at his brother as he spoke. Was this really his cold-hearted brother, who was also a huge menace to all mob, and underground organizations?

He was so shocked because Jacob hadn't ever been as communicating with his feelings as this. Not even when he had his greatest fallout with their father three years ago.

"Do you think it's the right time to tell her our feelings?" Jackson asked his brother, but Jacob was equally confused and hesitant. It wasn't because he wasn't certain of his feelings, but because London wasn't safe for anyone close to him or his family currently.

He took another puff as his mind wandered to last night's event, and what Christian had told him. He still wasn't certain if it was the Italians that he would be facing, or if there was another gang in London or close states that were stupidly messing with him. Either way, he was sure to find out tomorrow. So, it shouldn't be too soon if they tell her today, right?

"You should tell her for us, I believe you'd handle it better."

It took Anna roughly three hours to paint the image in her mind because she hadn't mastered drawing yet. She had always thought she could paint without mastering drawing but it only made her art harder to achieve.

"Maybe I should sign up for drawing tutorials." She mumbled to herself as she looked at the art she had drawn. Her eyes trailed along the edges of the painting as the brilliant rays of the radiant sun shone on it.

She was still looking at the piece, trying to figure out where to add finishing touches when she heard a gasp behind her. "This is beautiful..." Anna turned around to see Jacob behind her with a gaped jaw. He was flabbergasted as he stared at the stunning piece of art that Anna had just painted.

It was an illustration of two adolescents, who seemed to be interwoven with each other. They were holding hands but their backs were turned at each other. The most significant and captivating part of the drawing was that neither of the adolescents has a face or a graphical description of genitals that can differentiate their genders.

Looking at their long dark hair that was interlaced at the end, Jacob couldn't tell if they were males or females. "This is a masterpiece, Anna." He let out when he finally found his voice but it still came out breathless.

Anna's cheek flushed pink as he approached her, and she stood up nervously. She was aware that Jacob was a lover of art and might be able to discern the theme behind the art but regardless, she still wanted to let him see.

"Do you think I can sell if I want to?" She asked Jacob but he was still enthralled with the art before him.

"Are they twins?" He turned his head and raised a quizzical brow at Anna. The sun beamed on his dark hair, and at his gorgeous eyes, he looked so delicious and handsome that Anna couldn't help but swallow greedily.

Her brain momentarily turned foggy and she blinked at him. "U hm..." she couldn't remember what Jacob just asked until she heard Jackson's voice behind her.

"He said, are they twins like us?" This was the word Jackson heard as he entered the room. His eyes had gone straight to the painting, but he wasn't much of a lover of acts or painting unlike his brother, so he was also waiting for Anna's reply.

Anna shook her head, her eyes staring between the twins. Not deluding herself, she was aware that the twins might have run a few background checks on her, so she decided to tell them the truth. "This is an illustration of two female siblings." She let out frankly.

"It's really nice, wanna sell it to me?" Jacob asked and Anna's face lifted in a brilliant smile.

"Is it good enough to sell?" She asked, a hint of doubt in her voice even though she sounded excited.

"Of course, it is good. If you want to sell, you should auction it, and let enthusiastic art lovers like me bid for it. Then you will know how valuable your piece is." Jacob had a tentative smile on his face as he looked at Anna. "Instead of buying this, how about we make it your debut into the cultural industry? We will set up an art gallery for you and you can display and auction your pieces." He shared a look with his brother as he discussed a plan they had thought of with Anna.

It was meant to be a surprise but he was currently so overwhelmed by what their little woman had just created. He couldn't help but feel like she would be an outstanding talent in the cultural industry. As an art lover, he was excited to help her fulfil all her wishes regarding selling out her piece.

Anna blinked repeatedly upon listening to Jacob's words, she had to turn her head to Jackson to see if they shared the same intention. She was surprised to see him nodding and smiling at her as he walked closer to her.

Her heart beating wildly, she held the paintbrush in her hand against her chest to cease the thumbing, but it continued as Jackson spoke.

"Anna, do you want to go out with us? Not like a sex slave, or a plaything, but as our girlfriend, our woman."

Aww

Should I make this into a book?

Vema, the shore of the lewd, exists very close to the Verna, the flawless shore. These two lands are separated by a large magical water and they never crash. The shore of the lewd as its name implies contains the vulgar, filthy, and kinkiest people ever, while Verna's natives are innately and practically virtuous, innocent, and clean.

As this world never collides, no one knows anything at all about the other world, until Dirkna, a 19-year-old virgin, and a second-year student at Verna University accidentally teleported to Vema because of a single immoral thought.

Fortunately for him, he was bestowed a System by the Lewd Powerhouse upon his arrival, with the order that he must attempt and accomplish all sexual tasks given by the System, or else they would remove the System, and his innate virtuous body will be devoured by the lewd, erotic and lascivious aura in Vema.

This wasn't just a pardon for Dirkna, but also his only way of survival until he fulfilled all levels, and he was able to exist like a real local of Vema.

In Vema, there were no rules or restrainment for sexual activities, until the new leader, Lord Tema, from the house of Lust, one of the four prestigious houses of Vema, decreed that no one must get intimate with another forcefully. It was an absolute law, and not a person was above it. If caught, such an offender would be charged and compressed with the four different powerful lewd feelings until they bloat to death.

[Host, your virtuous body would soon be consumed by the overwhelming sensuality aura, if you don't activate the Lewd System, you will bloat to death.]

Dirkna throws his hand in the air in frustration and growls out loud. "I still have a day, don't I? That was what the Lords said." He barked at the Lewd System fixed inside him after it reminded him of its activation for the millionth time.

His eyes roaming around the location he was, Dirkna realizes that he was at the junction of the lane from the Powerhouse, and he was staring blankly at two junctions, with long tarred roads, which he cannot tell, the one that leads to The Lotus building. It was the apartment provided for him by the Lords of Vema until he completed his mission, and was able to exist in Vema.

"How about you do me a favor and point the way to The Lotus building instead of screeching in my head?" If Dirkna knew that the consequences of his single immoral act will bring him to Vema, the shore of the Lewd, he would have hidden his sexual thoughts in the deepest corner of his mind.

[Dear host, I have no active functions, as I have not been activated yet, and I cannot-

"Wait, is that not a car honk?" Excitement poured out of Dirkna's as he cut off his system words.

His dark eyes eagerly on the road, he saw a red Honda CRV racing towards him from the right junction. Excusing the driver's rough driving, Dirkna quickly moved away from the road before he died an untimely death.

"That- that driver definitely doesn't have a license." His voice trembled as he blurted out the moment he was able to breathe normally again. How can one -

His hand was on his chest, gently calming his panic-stricken self when this eyes widened in shock as he saw the car reversing.

Blinking away his fright, he swallowed his saliva and quickly turned his head to the other side awkwardly to avoid any interaction but the driver only found it more suspicious.

She squinted her brows, and her round eyes dilated with sexual desire as she checked Dirkna's tall, masculine frame, and side profile out. Where has such a goodie been hidden in Vema?

She licked her pink lips when she felt the lustful feeling rising in her core. With a small smile on her face, she adjusted her white V-neck pink top to expose her curvaceous waist and push out her huge chest.

After a glance at her rearview mirror, she decided to postpone her meeting with her father, and get acquainted with the stranger first.

Dirkna shivered slightly when he realized that the driver had parked, and it was a girl. Not just any girl, but the very one which he had never seen before. Peeping at her from the corners of his eyes, he stood upright with his hand in his pocket. He was trying not to notice how her waist was swaying as she walked towards him, and definitely not her chest which was almost spilling out.

When she got to a few feet before him, he still didn't raise or turn his head to look at her, making the female driver a bit mad. Is he proving hard to get? In the whole Vema, almost everyone wants to have a taste of her!

"Don't tell me you just entered your lascivious stage?" She ran her eyes all over him with a pitiful smirk on her face before she squinted her brows and quickly shook her head.

"You are not from here, are you?" From her assertive tone, Dirkna thought it wasn't a question, so he gradually nodded.

"What? You are not from Vema?" The female driver's shock increased when she heard him confirm her rhetorical question but she still didn't believe it.

She stood on her toes to grab Dirkna's chin, but he caught her hand before she could touch him.

"Don't touch me." He muttered cautiously, then quickly dropped her hand when it burned in his.

Groaning inwardly, he moved a step away from her to give a quality distance between them, but it only increased the female driver's wonder and persistent nature.

She was aroused by his voice and the innocence in it, but she still couldn't contain her amazement at the sight of a man, who was handsome as the devil, but calm and innocent as a dove.

"What? Are you joking? How can you not be from Vema?" She tried to get a glimpse of the handsome stranger she just found.

Appreciating a close-up of his facial figure, she felt her nipples tighten under her top, and the urge to pinch them right there before the man increased greatly in her.

Dirkna, who hadn't thought that the beautiful girl would continue staring at him, cleared his throat awkwardly to alert her but she smiled at him warmly.

[Host, no one can know that you are not originally from Vema or own a system, or else your virtuous body will be feasted and ravaged by anyone who could lay their hands on you.]

"Why didn't you tell me-

Dirkna gritted his teeth as he nearly spoke out his thoughts, and the female driver chuckled softly before stepping into his view, and then gently touching his chest. Her hands spread on his chest, Dirkna felt a strange rush of adrenaline running through his veins before he jumped away from her.

"I said, don't-

[Dear host, you have to act naturally, else you'd be suspected. If you are, you definitely wouldn't be able to make it to the next day before your body starts bloating from irresistible lust, passion, desire, and ardor]

Is this not a scam? How come it didn't tell him before? Dirkna never felt as dumbfounded like this before in his entire life.

"What's wrong with you? Why are you acting jittery?" The female driver frowned at Dirkna, "How old are you?" She asked curiously as she stepped away from him with her face filled with disapproval.

She didn't believe a full-grown man, who looked like a delicious candy, and the best she had ever seen would be underage.

When she moved away from him, Dirkna saw her chest jiggle, and his throat immediately felt dry. Why was he suddenly noticing every little thing about where it doesn't matter?

He should look at something else, but his mind currently has a mind of its own, and it's against his self-discipline.

"Are you acting dumb?" The female driver stares disapprovingly at the man before her when she caught him staring at her boobs after she thought he hadn't even reached his maturity age. "Vema men keep coming up with different tactics." She rolled her eyes with a pout. She wasn't anxious. The men she picks always end up in her bed.

Trying not to notice how seductive the female driver's brown eyes were, Dirkna shifted in his stance and bowed slightly toward her. His bow was short and graceful, like the high-borns of Verna, striking a remarkable interest in the female driver.

"I am Dirkna, can I know you?" His voice was low and pleasurable in her ears, but it was the usual greeting of the people of Verna, as the boys were taught from their childhood to treat women like jewels, and they cannot think about them or fantasies about them unless they were joined together in marriage.

A blush already rose on the female driver's face and she rubbed her thighs together to feel the wetness already between them.

Gently raising her head to look at Dirkna, she seductively smiled at him, she twirled her hair and replied. "I am Reema, do you want to know more than that?" Before she recalled that he had said Dirkna and not Dirkma.

Excerpt I can't wait to show y'all
II

This chapter was one the day Anna came back to London after five years. She became a very famous artist.

When Anna arrived at the restaurant she was to meet her client, she sent an email to her, and let her know that she had just gotten to the location.

Rebecca, who had been nursing her broken heart and wallowing in her unexplainable hatred for Anna, hadn't left her room after leaving Jackson's office that day, felt a rush of happiness surge through her when she received a message she had been expecting.

She had presumed that once the artist arrived and Jackson was able to get their contact information and also the art she was paid for, he would be appreciative toward her, and even tell his twin brother that she was the one that assisted him in finding the artist he was in search of.

Maybe, just maybe- she would be able to get the attention of Jacob Mikelson, and Jackson wouldn't think so bad of her anymore. He might be disgusted that she had done a bit of surgery to look like Anna, but his brother might find it attractive.

Rebecca had assumed she would be able to gain the twin's favor that way, so upon receiving Anna's email, she immediately screenshots it and sent them to Jackson's phone number before realizing that Jackson didn't know that she had his contact.

Jackson, on his way to the restaurant at a slow pace, was thinking of everything he and Jacob had talked about on their way from the airport. He hadn't been expecting the artist to arrive so soon, not foreseeing a personal message from Rebecca, was so shocked when Truecaller flashed out the name, Rebecca Cameron.

He had read the message before he recalled that he hadn't given her his number when she intruded on him that morning. So, how was she able to get his number? Jackson felt outraged at how close Rebecca Cameron was to him without him realizing it.

"Paige. That bitch!" He hit his hand harshly on the car steering wheel.

He immediately thought it must have been his ex-secretary that had leaked it to her, and he instantly forwarded her full name to one of his friends, who was also a CEO of a large company. Jackson made sure to tell him that Paige was a spy in his office, and who wouldn't be a good employee to anyone.

He didn't say anything aside from this, but he knew that Paige would never be employed in any big companies, and the lower company holders wouldn't dare to employ her for fear that they might be trampled upon.

Clearing that off his list, he added this to another crime that Rebecca had committed and began to blame himself for petitioning for her in front of Jacob.

"That filth- how dare her." He slammed his hand on the steering wheels in anger again as he geared up.

After waiting for a few minutes without her seeing any traces of her client, Anna decided that she couldn't wait with an empty stomach and ordered Pie and Mash, with a glass of Pinot Noir to go with it as she awaited her arrival.

As she was eating, she received a call from Maria, who told her that they had just arrived at her apartment, because Marcelo was hell-bent on eating Ice -cream.

"Aunt Maria, you are complaining." Marcelo's tiny yet firm voice sounded in Anna's ears and she chuckled softly.

"Oh, baby. I know I said I won't complain, and do everything you want but we went to five different Ice cream stores before we could find the flavor you like."

"Still you said-

"Okay, okay, Marcelo, you should thank your Aunt instead, how can you stress like that on your first day of meeting her ?" Anna scolded lightly as she imagined the little frown and pout her son would have on.

"Thank you, Aunt Maria." She heard Marcelo's voice as he appreciated Maria's effort and her heart warmed up.

Tears swelling in her eyes, she couldn't help but remember how scared she had been that she wouldn't be able to raise him as a good mother should. Looking back at how she had single-handedly raised her son into such a fine, docile, and smart little boy, the happiness in her heart was more profound than when she first received her first income.

"Anna, what would you like to eat, so we can have it ready before you come back?" Maria asked, and Anna's gaze went to the food she just ordered.

"Uhm, just something light. I just ordered some food here," She told Maria.

"You are eating? What about your client?" She asked, and Anna replied that they hadn't arrived yet.

"Wow, isn't that a bit rude? You came all the way from Jersey, and she couldn't even meet up with you in her borough?"

"I sent her an email when I got here, so she must be on her way," Anna said to Maria on the phone as she looked out of the restaurant to see a car pulling up. "Oh, I think she just arrived. I will call you when I'm done, okay?"

"Alright then,"

"Kiss Marcelo for me please," Anna muttered quickly before she hung up to watch her client appear.

Just before the car opened Anna heard a voice call her attention, and she turned around to see the waitress, who had brought her order beside her. "How can I help you?" She asked when she remembered that she had paid for the meal.

"Uh, Ma'am, that customer asked this to be delivered to you." She smiled awkwardly as she delivered a plate of strawberry cake to Anna.

Anna raised her head to see that the customer was already approaching. He was a young man with a beanie over his shoulder height braids, he had on a matching hood with joggers, and he was fairly handsome.

"Uhm- " Anna blinked before she cleared her throat and politely rejected the cake, "sorry, I'm waiting on my client here and she just arrived." She turned to look at the window for her client again only to see the back view of a man walking in.

Anna gritted her teeth when she realized it wasn't her client, but the customer had reached her table, and there was no way she could avoid that scenario anymore.

"Hello, beautiful, can I occupy this seat?" The young man asked, and Anna groaned inwardly when the waitress left to attend to other customers.

She knew if this was 5 years ago, she wouldn't have even been able to leave home and to talk to meeting up with anyone. But after everything in Jersey, she had learned enough social skills to politely refuse any man.

"No gentleman, you can't. I have a meeting with a client here, and she will be arriving soon."

These words of hers strolled into Jackson's ears and his body trembled at how familiar the voice was.

Anna? Is that you? He muttered under his breath as he quickened his pace.

"Look, lady. You should just accept while I ask nicely." The young man flashed Anna the knife he had fastened under his hoodie and she gasped in terror.

"I- uhm-" She stuttered before her eyes fell on Jackson, who was right behind the young man.

Anna's eyes widened in shock and she literally saw her life flash in fright before Jackson grabbed the young man's hands and held it up behind his back.

"How dare you threaten my woman?" His voice was filled with years of rage, irritation, heartbreak, agony, and distress as he growled.

The commotion attracted other customers and they started looking at Anna's table curiously with their phones to record before the waitresses and the restaurant manager arrived.

Even with their appearance, Jackson didn't let go of the young man but instead wrapped his two hands with one of his large strong ones to get the knife under his hoodie.

As he brought out the knife, he knocked him unconscious, and Jackson's eyes trailed to see Anna taking slow breaths as she stared blankly at him.

"Sir, we will take-

The manager's words got stuck in his throat when Jackson turned his cold face to look at him. "Mi...mi..kelson." He stuttered as he swallowed in fear because he had thought that it was Jacob.

Without sparing him another glance, he took a picture of the young man before moving to Anna and carrying her in a bridal style.

Anna, who hadn't expected that to be his next action, was too shocked to react, and before she could, he was already taking her out of the restaurant.

"Jackson, listen. I came here to meet a client, she will be arriving soon, you cannot just take me with you." She hit him on the chest but Jackson couldn't hear any of her words after she called him 'Jackson'

"I am Jackson to you now, is that it? Is that what five years have done to you?" The pain in his voice cut through Anna and she almost swallowed back her resistance.

"We will talk about this later, I can't just leave. I have a client to deliver a parcel to." She hit his chest with her hand repeatedly again but he didn't put her down.

Gritting his teeth, Jackson gently dropped Anna beside the restaurant's entrance door, and she heaved a long sigh before taking her time to look at him.

Same time, Jackson was also looking at her, and he felt the pain he had stuck away rushing back into his heart with great force.

"Jackson, I- uhm."

The first thing that came up in Anna's mind as she started at Jackson was her baby, Marcelo, and she instantly told herself that once she was able to get away from Jackson now, she will take the next flight back to Jersey.

"What is the name of the client you are waiting for?" Jackson asked, trying his best not to look as heartbroken as he felt after meeting Anna again.

"Rebecca Cameron, she was to-

Anna hadn't finished her words when Jackson hurled her off her feet again.

"Jackson, hey hey. HEY!!!"

Y'all should check my wall before I cry

Last Chapter of Not The Daddies She Expected

"None of your business." Jacob replied impatiently as his eyes trailed to the driver that had come with their mother before turning back to her.

"We are on our way out, you can come along if you are here as our mother, and not your husband's wife."

"Jacob." Jackson cautioned slightly even though he was also currently angry at their parents.

Sighing, he used the remote in his hands to open the door. "Mother, we just received news that Anna's father is dead, and we are on our way to see her family." Jackson explained calmly to their mother, intentionally hiding the fact that their son was also there, to see her reaction.

Rose looked away from Jacob's cold face as she heard the news about Anna's father's death. She almost couldn't believe that the man her husband was talking to on the phone less than a few hours was already dead.

She couldn't bring herself to feel anything for him, but she was so concerned about Anna after everything she had heard. Without saying a word, she moved closer to Jacob and tenderly pulled Anna into her embrace.

"I will wait with her here, she doesn't have to go and see him." Rose asserted as raised her eyes at her boys, but Anna shook her head, and gently pulled away from her.

This was her first reaction after 20 minutes, and they all looked at her as she spoke in a firm voice. "No, I want to see him," she swallowed what she was sure was something like tranquillity descended on her after so many years.

"I will get the car." Jackson broke the short silence after Anna's words before he turned to get the car.

Jacob didn't even say a word to his mother before he pulled Anna back into his arms. "Did your husband know you are here?" He threw another question at her but she scowled at him as she stared at his beard.

"Look at how you look older than your father? People will think you are Jackson's older brother and not the other way around."

Jacob frowned at his mother's joke but his heart felt a bit warm with her presence.

"Your father said to come and accompany you boys since I miss you so much. It's nice knowing that none of you miss me. I should have gone to Rhoda instead." The fake scowl on her face got bigger as she added.

Jacob had almost believed her words until he saw the expression on her driver's face. "So, you fight with your husband, is that it?" He asked, and Rose was about to deny it when Jacob's phone rang in his pocket.

"Good, take her and her father back to their house quietly and report a case of arson when you are done," Jacob said after he heard that the remaining Camerons had been found, and also the most recent crime of Rebecca Cameron.

"Find those boys and round them up too," those bloody bastards that had also accepted her deal should be burnt along with her and her father.

Rose and Anna furrowed their brows curiously at Jacob as they listened to him.

"Bring my mother along with us," Jacob said to Rose's driver after Jackon returned, then wrapped his hand around Anna's waist before he turned to enter the car again.

When they all got to Anna's childhood house, she swallowed when she saw the police and some other people around it.

Anna felt her heart throb with ache when she saw her sister, who had been very cheerful a few hours ago, now disheveled and distraught.

There was sadness in her heart as she couldn't share her grief. Yeah, the man that had just died was her biological father too, but she couldn't bring herself to mourn him. If she was feeling anything in her heart right now, it would be serenity, and despair for her sister.

Her heart, which was always in a state of fidgety anytime she remembered that her father would rather ruin her life than watch her be happy, finally felt at peace after 7 years.

Maria noticed the two expensive cars almost immediately when they arrived, and she didn't have to guess twice to know that it was her sister that had arrived. Swallowing back her brief, she saw Adrian give her a warm smile a few steps away from her and she sniffed back her tears.

It was hard for her as she was really close to Mr. Walton, and he had been a good father to her. Excuse the fact that he hates it when she talks about Anna.

"Are you ready to go down?" Jacob asked and Anna nodded, she had seen Adrian too, but she hadn't seen the sight of her son, which she was greatly grateful for.

When they got down, Rose didn't, as she had already asked the police if the deceased was inside the house, and they had said that his remains had been transferred to the morgue.

Anna walked quietly towards Maria, zero expression on her face as she approached the house that she had lived in for 18 years before she was given by her father to his old creditor.

"Anna." Maria called out before she met her halfway, and then both started wailing softly in each other's arms. Each of them cried for a different reason as they consoled themselves.

That night, Anna once again slept peacefully between the twins, and Marcelo woke up the next morning to see two familiar older men before him.

Of course, he was able to instantly recognize them as his fathers after the painting, and the fact that Jacob had shaved off his beard that morning made them easier to identify.

A small smirk raised on his lip, and Jacob almost cracked up in laughter. "Did he just smirk at me?"

"I think it's a good start." Jackson asserted humorously, looking at the little boy, who was now climbing from the bed that he was sure he didn't sleep in.

"I want to see mommy." Marcelo said to the twins, his little voice was energetic and clear.

Jackson and Jacob shared a smile as they heard their son's voice for the first time.

"Did you know who we are, little man?" Jacob asked as he squatted to Marcelo's height.

His dark eyes roamed the boy's face and he felt a strange feeling in his heart before he heard Marcelo's little voice again.

"My daddies?"

Jackson and Jacob laughed after hearing his words of acknowledgment, "don't let your mommy hear that." Jacob let out and they laughed again.

Marcelo pouted after listening to them laugh at him repeatedly, but when he remembered that his mother had called them his fathers, and not daddies, he corrected himself.

"Good boy." Jackson stroked his rough hair and Marcelo beamed happily at them.

"Let's go and see your mommy." The twins said in sync and the little boy left with them.

It was the next morning, around 11 am, but Anna hadn't woken up yet.

Yesterday was a major turning point in all their lives, especially Anna, and she could finally rest, as she had confronted everything she had once been terrified of for so many years in just one night.

When the twins arrived in the master room with Marcelo, he was slightly shocked that she was still fast asleep. "Mommy?" He had to rush to her to believe that she was actually sleeping.

With the arrival of Rose, of course, there would be changes everywhere in Jackson's simple mansion, especially his empty kitchen.

Immediately she woke up early in the morning, she had called the head of the chefs from the main house to report to Jackson's house. She ordered her to come with, and also buy on her way more than enough foodstuff, as she wasn't really a fan of takeout like her sons.

This was when Luciano found out everything and also Marcelo's existence. Over the night, he had greatly missed his wife as this would be the first night he would be sleeping alone, making him reflect on his previous actions.

"If not for you, Mr. Walton would probably be in the house, drinking his alcohol and not dead, you know this," Rose said to her husband on the call, and he sighed heavily.

Last night, he had realized so many times, and one of it was that he was getting old. He might still have the eagerness to run everything like he was a youth, but he didn't have a new-age intelligence and also strength anymore.

"I apologized for everything already, Roseline." He admitted his guilt again, his voice on the phone showing every bit of remorse that he felt.

"Apology must be given to whom it is due. You should apologize to Anna, her sister, and also your sons. You can't do this on the phone, you have to come down here and do the necessary, so Jacob would still allow Marcelo to call you grandfather."

"I doubt that." Luciano said as he chuckled softly as he heard his wife's last words.

"Anyways, get here as soon as you can."

"I will be on my way."

After Rose dropped the call with her husband, she turned to see Rhoda and Christian behind her.

"I presume that's uncle," Rhoda said to Rose, her composure was a bit better than yesterday.

She had heard about David and the unexpected arson that had claimed the lives of his sister, and his father.

She had thought it was just an accident, but Christian had told her that it was arranged by Jacob.

"Hello, Rose." Christian greeted calmly with respect.

Rose smiled warmly at him in reply and then at the grown woman beside him, who she had practically raised like her daughter. "Amore mio."

"Aunt, I can't believe you are actually here," Rhoda flew into Rose's hands and they both embraced each other affectionately.

"I also need to apologize to Anna and my brothers," she said to her aunt-in-law and Rose gently patted her hands.

She had heard from Jackson about Rhoda's contribution to all of this but she couldn't blame her.

Rose was also aware of what Rhoda had to sacrifice to finally marry the man of her choice, and everything she had to endure after her honeymoon, so she understood her perfectly.

"I'm sure they will be out soon." Rose asserted before leading them back to the living room.

"Hmm..." Anna rubbed her hand on her closed eyes as she gradually woke up from sleep.

Her half-closed eyes falling on Marcelo, she grins before pulling him to her gently. "Marcey baby, why did you wake up so early today." She grunted softly as she sprayed peppered kisses on his gorgeous face.

"Mommy, you are the one that slept so long," Marcelo replied, before pointing at Jacob and Jackson that had been along with him for Anna to finally wake up from her long sleep.

The last time the twins had seen her sleep so long was after that night they had come back from Sodom when she got divorced by her ex-husband.

"Uhm," Anna's body shuddered as she watched the twins approach her with their eyes filled with love and adoration in their eyes.

Her eyes moved back to Marcelo, who also had a huge smile on his small face. That was when Anna knew that she had gotten everything she had ever wanted, and more, and if there was anything in the future that would terrify her, she would easily overcome it with these three men beside her.

The End.

Not an update!!! Steamy Christmas book?

After listening to Dallas's words, sexual excitement ran through me, and I gently rub his dick, moving my hand around it up and down.

"Ah," he dragged his breath between his teeth, and his long lashes fluttered as he looked at me.

Dallas moaned and groaned in my ears when I moved closer and unevenly rubbed my breasts on his chest while bobbing his erect dick.

I could barely feel it a few minutes ago, but it's now hard against his boxer like it couldn't wait to escape its captive.

You should stop now. This teasing is going too far.

I reminded myself but my body already grew a mind after listening to Dallas's desirable groans and moans.

It was like encouragement in my head, telling me to do more. Make him groan more.

I was losing control of myself while I was pleasuring him and it was an insane sexual attraction I'd never felt.

My clitoris was on fire. It was throbbing so hard at the moment, aching for a touch... his touch, just a brush, but I couldn't... I couldn't let it happen because it would be another whole thing.

"Ava," Dallas moaned out my name, and I breathed out heavily. "Ahh, fuckk." His sensual raspy voice made its way to my brain, and it got muddy with intense pleasure.

Slowly, I dragged his boxer down, and my eyes rolled into the back of my head when I cupped his hard, thick, and long dick with my hand.

A gasp escaped my throat, and I felt a sticky liquid dripping down my thighs.

I watched him breathe heavily as he shook his head at me. I knew he was telling me that this was getting deeper, but I was enjoying this too much to stop. This erotic feeling was strange to me. I was tormented and encouraged by how he was looking at me like he couldn't wait to tear my vagina with his dick, and how his dark half-eyes twinkled every time his dick jerked in my hand.

I licked my lips and continued bobbing my hand on his dick, my thumb on the tip as I rubbed the sticky cum on it and all around the edges then down his thick length.

He was getting harder and harder. At one point my fogged, sexually awoken brain couldn't take it anymore, and my legs inside the water started shivering due to extreme pleasure.

"I want to touch you so bad," I heard Dallas's voice in my head before he gently moved his hand to my waist inside the water, and pinned my back to the edge of the skimming pool.

"Can I return the teasing?" He asked, his eyes locked with mine, and my nipples thickened with lust under my bra.

I was aching so badly, and my brain was feeling muddled with sexual imagery, which include him raising my legs and wrapping them around his slim torso, while his dick that was currently poking my thighs slipped inside me.

It had been so long.

So long since I felt a man's penetration and I only have to nod. I only have to make any gesture at all, and he will be inside me.

Dallas was staring intensely at me, waiting for any reply from me, but I couldn't.

My body was raging with hunger, craving, and starvation but I couldn't give to my sexual appetite. This was wrong. Everything... It would be wrong of me to make use of him this way. Like a toy.

When I started telling myself to heed rational thinking and not my lecherous body, my brain started getting clearer, and I breathed out before slowly pushing him away to put a distance between us.

"We should get back to the party," I said to him and he looked at me for a while before nodding and dipping his head back into the pool.

Fuck. What have I done? I groaned inwardly as I watched his body graciously move in the clear water and within a few minutes, he was climbing out of the pool in his boxers with a semi-hard dick.

When he didn't turn back to look at me, I heaved a deep sigh before I started swimming out of the pool too.

check my works

CPSIA information can be obtained
at www.ICGtesting.com
Printed in the USA
LVHW042011130123
736977LV00013B/883